WISDOM FROM MOUNT ATHOS

A companion volume to
The Monk of Mount Athos
also available from SVS Press

Wisdom from Mount Athos

The Writings of Staretz Silouan
1866–1938

by

ARCHIMANDRITE SOPHRONY

translated from the Russian by
Rosemary Edmonds

ST VLADIMIR'S SEMINARY PRESS
CRESTWOOD, NEW YORK

Library of Congress Cataloging-in-Publication Data

Siluan, monk, 1866-1938.
   Wisdom from Mount Athos: the writings of Staretz Silouan, 1866-1938/
   [compiled] by Archimandrite Sophrony, translated from the Russian by
   Rosemary Edmonds.
      p. cm.
   Originally published: Crestwood, N.Y.: St. Vladimir's Press,
   1874.
      I. Spiritual life—Orthodox Eastern Church.   I. Sofronii,
Archimandrite, 1896-   II. Title
BX382 .S5 2000
248.4'819—dc21   00-062561
ISBN-13: 978-0-913836-17-0
ISBN-10: 0-913836-17-6

WISDOM FROM MOUNT ATHOS

ST VLADIMIR'S SEMINARY PRESS
575 Scarsdale Road, Crestwood, NY 10707
www. svspress. com • 1-800-204-2665

ISBN 978-0-913836-17-0

Contents

Foreword

'Him that cometh to me I will in no wise cast out.'

In this spirit the Holy Mountain greeted Staretz Silouan, just as it had greeted pilgrims throughout the centuries. The Elders, none the less, generally like to test how serious the newcomer is in his desire to become a monk. But in the majority of monasteries and hermitages preliminary inquiries are so perfunctory that anyone who has made up his mind, and is resolute, manages to stay. Inasmuch as monasticism entails, above all, a consciousness of one's sinfulness and consequent need for repentance, there can be nothing in a man's past that could make him unacceptable in the monastery. It does happen occasionally that a monk, who insisted in the beginning, proves by his later conduct that he did not understand what he was doing when he arrived on Mount Athos; but the vast majority are men who came with a burning desire for God. They came in fear of God and, I believe, found what they sought.

It is not unusual for a school of thought, a nation, even an empire to be justified by individual people of high attainment, whose luminous achievements for humanity qualify and impart glory to whole epochs, History shutting its eyes to all the sombre, negative factors of the period. Judged after this fashion, the Holy Mountain must rank high in the annals of mankind for having given the world saints without number in the course of its thousand years' of existence - saints who, as Christ said, are the salt of the earth.

Life on Mount Athos is unique, unlike life anywhere else on earth. The Holy Mountain is a kingdom of monks, with those who are not monks - agricultural labourers, government functionaries, pilgrims and the like - there only temporarily. The 'citizens' of this monastic kingdom, at the present time about a thousand, have declined in number since the First World War. In 1912 the Russian monastery of St Panteleimon, to which Staretz Silouan belonged, had almost two thousand monks out of a general population of some nine thousand. Created for a great multitude of Orthodox monks, without regard to nationality, the religious community of Mount Athos represents the universal nature of Orthodoxy and has borne rich fruit.

The profound feeling for religion of many Russians not infrequently reaches such a pitch of intensity that the soul can find no satisfaction in the hallowed institution of marriage and must seek the widest possible freedom to give herself wholly to God the way of monasticism. Russians who went to Mount Athos did not concern themselves with any theological justification for their chosen life of spiritual struggle. The example of the apostles and countless other saints down the centuries of the Church's history, and first and foremost of Christ Himself, precluded all hesitation. Over and over again fellow-monks told me that they had left their native land like Abraham, who received the injunction to get him out of his country, and from his kindred, to go in search of the city and kingdom which is not of this world - the 'continuing city'. Such a one was Staretz Silouan.

Certainly, many Russian ascetics, albeit of the first rank elected to seek salvation in Russia rather than anywhere else. After eight years on the Holy Mountain, Paissy Velichkovsky decided to return to Moldavia with many of his disciples and Vlachs. Seraphim Sarovsky, according to a certain abbot Makarios, preferred Holy Russia to Mount Athos. The famous shepherd of souls, Archpriest John of Krondstadt, together with various other eminent Russian ascetics, likewise chose to stay in the spiritual world of Russia.

Geographically, the Holy Mountain is not far from the great centres of civilisation but the very fact that throughout the centuries the life of its inhabitants has differed radically from life outside has cut Mount Athos off from the rest of the world. This isolation, coupled with the profound stillness of nature all around, favours prayer of the deep heart and thought of the great calm in the Kingdom to come. The slow eastern rhythm of Athonite life - in absolute contrast to the stupefying beat of our contemporary mechanised existence - adds a precious ingredient of spiritual comfort to this chosen place, since it helps one to forget the temporal and plunge into contemplation of eternal mysteries.

The vast majority of monks begin soon after their arrival on the Holy Mountain to sense the sanctity of the place and become aware of the ascetic traditions of Orthodox monasticism. Their reverent confidence in the heritage of the Holy Fathers goes so deep that most of them remain for ever attached even to intrinsically unimportant details or customs. Hence their dread of any reform or novelty whatever. This could be variously accounted for but my attention, during the whole of my time among monks in monasteries and in the 'desert', was stayed not so much on the outward form of life as on an effort to penetrate to the spirit at the core of the ascetic tradition of Athonite monasticism. I considered it vital to turn away from externals lest these externals, either by their beauties or their defects, screened the true knowledge that lay behind. My urge to understand was the fiercer because I had come to Mount Athos persuaded that here was the place to learn the Gospel life.

The Athonite monk is convinced beyond doubt that the Orthodox Church is privileged with the most authentic knowledge of the One True God. The way to the Father lies uniquely through the Son, only-begotten and consubstantial with the Father. He, and He alone, 'knows the Father' with complete knowledge, and 'no man cometh unto the Father, but by the Son'. Knowledge is acquired through prayer of the mind united with the heart, and our whole being given over to God. The heart is the spiritual centre of the human personality and the mind is enlightened through the heart. The monk knows the travail of launching the mind in the heart. But he knows, too, that this secret realm cannot be entered painlessly, and so he embarks willingly on the ascetic struggle. When the roots of the Tree of Life press into the human heart the monk feels a sort of spiritual pain. In many ways suffering of the spirit is unlike physical suffering. Spiritual pain is the source of the energy needed to resist the pull of earthly attractions for the sake of that other divine and eternal world. Through this form of asceticism we may discover the hidden meaning of the apparent paradoxes of the Beatitudes - Blessed are the poor in spirit; Blessed are they that mourn; Blessed are they which are persecuted; and so on. Just as in the scientific world approximation to the infinitely small started the conquest of cosmic space, so approach to the divine mysteries lies through humility and the kind of *kenosis* that we see in Christ, Who 'made himself of no reputation'.

The fruits of ascetic striving are not only prayer in the heart: the mind is imbued with the knowledge expressed in a supremely condensed form in the dogmas of the Church. And only through the union of prayer and knowledge does life in God become fuller and more perfect. Prayer by itself is not yet perfection. And intellectual familiarity with dogmas is not perfection either. Hence the Athonite's twofold determination to cling to prayer and preserve the dogmatic teaching inherited from the Fathers of the Church.

Occasionally, this stern repudiation of extraneous influences is reinforced by an instinctive aversion having its roots in the past. At the time of the Crusades representatives of Rome sought with fire and sword to suppress Orthodoxy and impose on the East, firstly, the universal supremacy of the Roman bishop and, secondly, the Roman Catholic doctrine concerning the Trinity. Many Athonite monks were tortured and burnt alive for their refusal to submit to the Roman Pope. And since then the very life-blood of the monastic inhabitants of the Holy Mountain has been suffused with the memory of those cruelties, so that a great and ever-present dread persists of all contact with a Rome of that kind. This explains their stubborn resistance to absolutely everything, significant or insignificant, which proceeds from the Vatican, and their resolute opposition to any of their own ecclesiastical dignitaries with leanings towards Rome.

This determined rejection by the Orthodox monks of Mount Athos of those of their hierarchs willing to converse with the papacy is accounted for partly by the fact that the Orthodox world recognises that it is not only for the hierarchy to preserve holy traditions and true understanding of the revelation in regard to Divine Being, but for the whole people of the Church.

It is in no wise possible to approve the arrogant element in this attitude towards patriarch or bishop - an attitude which can stifle their activity and paralyse all initiative. But it does denote the ordinary churchman's awareness of his freedom. Orthodox believers do not doubt that they are living members of the Church, with responsibility for preserving her in the way of truth. This means that historically the Orthodox Church is always faced with the extraordinarily difficult task of uniting the principle of *'Sobornost'* as an ontological attribute of the Church with the 'personalism' in which she raises her children, and to which she must lead them.

All down the ages the Fathers of the Church have fought for Orthodoxy, straining to apprehend Revelation in all its pleroma and integrity. It is not easy to realise this high purpose that the Christian East sets itself. Nevertheless, it is not right to deny this purpose since the inevitable result of denial would be the gradual reduction of the root content of the Revelation that has been given to us, with a consequent loss of faith itself. Interpreting as she does the principle of the Person—Hypostasis in Divine Being as the bearer of the whole fulness of this Being, the Church seeks from man, as the image of God, the plenitude of love about which Staretz Silouan speaks with such emphasis. Monks who lack this universal love fail the Church by not bringing into her life the deeper knowledge and greater holiness expected of them. (But, needless to say, the higher the ideal the more elusive it is.)

If we appreciate the cause of the almost continual tension between the different trends in the Orthodox Church, we shall see that the *Sobornost* of the Church requires from her members an incomparably wider experience than they have arrived at. In order to be a true member of the Church, each of the faithful must humbly recognise both his own responsibility and his inadequacy, and be ever watchful to accept each and every one as a potential channel for the Holy Spirit. Inspiration from on High does not inevitably depend on hierarchical status. It is not automatically controlled by priority of rank. And every time human passions appear in the place of a prayerful waiting on the action of grace, perfection of unity remains impossible, and an intellectual or psychological struggle sets in between the members of the Assembly.

The Athonite monk devotes his main strength to the prayer of the mind in the heart, which demands unflagging effort. This pressure to 'pray without ceasing' does not facilitate theological research. He therefore prefers some simple occupation which will not require a great deal of thought but will leave him free to combine work with keeping his mind intent in the heart. It follows naturally that the monks of Mount Athos feel themselves unfitted for the intellectual dialogue of oecumenical gatherings. At the same time they cannot help remarking their opponents' frequent ignorance in the domain of mental prayer. They see that the culture of the heart is foreign to them and that they tend to pray mostly from the head. The Orthodoxy of the Holy Mountain and Roman Catholicism are two fundamentally different worlds. And so far their fusion is unthinkable.

Today there is a certain renaissance of Athonite monasticism in the sense that a score or so of new arrivals on the Holy

Mountain have a theological formation. But the purpose of this study is to describe Mount Athos as it was in Staretz Silouan's day.

Until I settled in the 'desert' I did not really know the life of the Holy Mountain as a whole. It was only when I became spiritual counsellor to four monasteries and a great number of hermitages and isolated hermits that the hidden kernel of this astonishing place was opened up to me. I encountered seven monks to whom the vision of uncreated light had been vouchsafed - and there were surely others whom I did not hear of. I am eternally thankful to Providence for allowing me the undeserved happiness of living among such ascetics for twenty-two years. But the most important event in my life was to meet with Staretz Silouan who, after Christ's appearance to him, never ceased imploring God to grant to all mankind to know Him through the Holy Spirit. His attitude to other confessions was both courteous and liberal. There was no disdain; people must be allowed to serve God in their own fashion, although, as is crystal-clear from his writings, he himself was heart and soul devoted to the Orthodox Church, and totally integrated with Orthodoxy.

It was the Staretz who resolved perplexities which had long confronted me, and helped me, as had none of my other mentors, gradually to find answers to the problems with which I was engrossed - how, for instance, living in this world, can one avoid sin? How can we be certain that the spirit operating in us is the Holy Spirit proceeding from the Father? Since man is called to create, what is the noblest form of creative work? What state of our spirit indicates that we truly are the image of the Living God?

I have not retained to the full and made my own anything of what I learned from the Staretz, and therefore have no right to discourse on these things. But let the partial knowledge which was somehow revealed to me in the Staretz' lifetime, through the strength of his prayer, serve as a basis for what follows.

To consider briefly the first of the above points - how to avoid sin. Christ disclosed this mystery of the holy life to Staretz Silouan when He bade him, 'Keep thy mind in hell, and despair not'. Immediately I heard from the Staretz that the *Lord Himself* had taught him how sin could be conquered, my reverence for him and complete belief in his saintliness convinced me that this utterance really had come from Christ Himself. And I tried to apply the prescript to my own life.

To contemplate the holiness of God and realise one's own total unworthiness to be united for ever with such a God appals the spirit. The knowledge that we are in thrall to all the sins makes us despair. Then is our prayer filled with weeping. When we thus sentence ourselves to hell we are divested of all that is earthly and temporal, since only eternity lies before us. Sin is arrested: there is no more pride, no hatred, no fear; no seeking for glory, riches or power. Only the peril of falling into ever-lasting despair. But, reaching this point, we stop: 'and despair not'. And if we continue aware of our dishonour, a state of mind which corresponds to fact, we thereby enable the Spirit of Truth, Who proceeds from the Father, to relate to our hearts.

Afterwards, reading the Gospel with careful attention, I remarked a certain similarity between the Lord's command to Staretz Silouan and the mode He adopted for Himself here on earth. Christ never sinned - 'The prince of this world . . . hath nothing in me' - so there is no identity between Him and us; but there is undoubtedly an analogy. Christ's whole life, as the true Son of man, in all things like unto us, even to the point of allowing Satan to tempt Him, shows us how it is possible to over-come every sin. ('For in that he himself hath suffered being tempted, he is able to succour them that are tempted.') In following His teaching and His example we find that we are delivered from the energy in us of sinful passions - pride and despair depart from our hearts. We know from the Staretz' writings that when he did as Christ counselled, his mind would enter the sphere of PURE prayer, and within his heart the Spirit of God would witness to salvation and grant him to live a kind of resurrection.

'Keep thy mind in hell, and despair not.' This is the highway to the world of divine holiness.

To turn now to my second question - how can we be sure that the spirit within us is indeed the Third Hypostasis of the Holy Trinity, and not something else? St John the Divine warns us, 'Believe not every spirit, but try the spirits whether they are of God'. This is of vital importance to every one of us. According to Staretz Silouan's doctrine, the Holy Spirit gave him to know the Divinity of Christ; in the Holy Spirit he knew God. The consubstantiality of the Son and the Holy Spirit is further discerned from the fact that when the Spirit, proceeding from the Father, does indeed visit the soul, the soul experiences the whole content of the teaching and commandments of Christ. Therefore, if the spirit within us speaks in full accord with the Gospel commandments, then verily it is the Holy Spirit. Thus the Son and the Holy Spirit bear mutual witness. The Holy Spirit is the Light of eternal life; the breath of the Holy Spirit in us is the power of divine love, inspiring the soul with deep compassion for all, including enemies. And the soul feels this gentle, compassionate love for enemies through the action of the Holy Spirit as an entirely natural state in which all inner conflict is extinguished and divine harmony reigns.

So long as man continues to be subject to death, he remains without power to love those who imperil his life or well-being. Consequently, love for enemies, the love commanded of us by Christ, the love of which Staretz Silouan speaks, is a passage from death unto life eternal, whereby the soul is assured of the ultimate victory of Christ's love.

Many-sided is the image of God in man. Man's creative power is one aspect, manifesting itself in various spheres and branches of culture - civilisation, art, science, and so forth. This creative power does not rest here but continues to transcend the visible and temporal in its striving to attain to the origin of all that exists - God the Creator.

Having in the beginning made man without collaboration on the part of man, God has never since done anything with man without enlisting his co-operation. The natural world is so arranged that man is constantly faced with problems to which he must seek solutions. But in order truly to work with God in the creation of the world man must ever aspire to the utmost possible knowledge of God Himself. The continual climb towards further and further knowledge of God is also a creative act, though of an especial order. My talks with Staretz Silouan concentrated, of course, on prayer and living according to God's will; but my previous career naturally inclined me to reflect on creative work in general, and its meaning. In my young days, through a Russian painter who afterwards became famous, I had been attracted to the idea of pure creativity, taking the form of abstract art. This engrossed me for two or three years and led to the first theological thought to originate within my own mind. Just as every artist apprehends objective reality through the forms and modes of his art, so I derived ideas for my abstract studies from life around me. I would look at a man, a house, a plant, at intricate machinery, extravagant shadowscapes on walls or ceilings, at quivering bonfire flames, and would compose them into abstract pictures, creating in my imagination visions that were not like actual reality. This was how I interpreted the teaching of my master - not to copy natural phenomena but to produce new pictorial facts. Fortunately, I soon realised that it was not given to me, a human being, to create from 'nothing', in the way only God can create. I realised that everything that I created was conditioned by what was already in existence. I could not invent a new colour or line that had never existed anywhere before. An abstract picture is like a string of words, beautiful and sonorous in themselves, perhaps, but never expressing a complete thought. In

13

short, an abstract picture represented a disintegration of being, a falling into the void, a return to the *non esse* from which we had been called by the creative act of God. I therefore abandoned my fruitless efforts to devise something entirely new, and the problem of creative work now became closely linked in my mind with the problem of cognition of Being. The whole world, practically every visual scene, became mysterious, uncommonly beautiful, profound. Light changed, to caress and surround objects with a halo, as it were, of glory, imparting to them vibrations of life impossible for the artist to depict with the means at his disposal. I was filled then with reverent worship for the First Craftsman, the Creator of all things, and a longing to meet Him, learn from Him, know how He created.

Talking with the Staretz fixed my attention on the Person of Christ: how did He, the Son of man, act? 'The Son can do nothing of himself, but what he seeth the Father do: for what so ever he doeth, these also doeth the Son likewise. For the Father loveth the Son, and sheweth him all things that himself doeth.' But the only-begotten Son, became the Son of man, became in all things like us. Therefore everything that He said about the Son of man, about Himself, can apply to each one of us. And so if the Father loves us, it follows that He will show us all things that He doeth and in what manner. This means that in the last analysis all of us are called to collaborate in the eternal creative act of the Father. It is proper to man to aspire to perfection, to wish to enter into the living stream of divine eternity whither the Christ-Man was the first to go.

Thus, where creative work is concerned, in his ultimate search man gradually abandons all that is relative and temporal, in order to attain undying perfection. On this earth perfection, to be sure, is never absolute. And yet we may call them perfect who speak only what is given to them by the Spirit, in imitation of Christ Who said, 'I do nothing of myself; but as my Father hath taught me, I speak these things'.

This creative work is the noblest of all work available to man. Man sets out, not passively but in a creative spirit, towards this ideal, but always remembering to avoid any tendency to create God after his own image.

I was also deeply preoccupied by the problem of how we, so narrow and circumscribed, can possibly apprehend that we are the image of the Almighty God, God all-containing, all-excelling. Here Staretz Silouan was my salvation. He would tell me that if one devoutly tries to keep Christ's commandments, the soul will be filled with the grace of the Holy Spirit; and then with deep compassionate love one prays for the whole world as for oneself, and longs for every man's well-being rather than for one's own. We are taught that Christ's prayer in the garden of Gethsemane encompassed the whole human race, from the first Adam to the last child to be born of woman. The prayer that the Staretz prescribed can undoubtedly be likened to this all-redeeming prayer of the Lord, and it therefore triumphs over the limitations of the individual. Such prayer is a transition into another dimension - the dimension of the person-hypostasis, in the likeness of the Hypostasis of the Word made flesh. We know that to the extent that man becomes like unto Christ in his earthly life, so he is already divinised and made a communicant in Divine life.

The realisation from personal experience that any change in my intellectual conception of Divine Being inevitably affected my whole life showed me that every confession or form of mysticism has its own specific spirituality. For this reason I feel absolutely convinced that the entire character of Staretz Silouan's ascetic life belongs to the world of the Orthodox Church. He himself wrote, after a certain father had argued that all heretics would perish, 'I do not know about that. But I believe only in the Orthodox Church. In her is the joy of salvation through Christ-like humility'. The life of each and every Christian confession is conditioned at all levels by its conception of the Holy Trinity. Differences in theological interpretation of the principle of the

Person-Hypostasis in the Divine Being constitute a watershed, a demarcation line, not only between the various religions but between the sundry Christian confessions too. Unhappily, most contemporary theologians have not yet grasped this, though it is far and away the chief point that ought to be resolved.

'Every one that is of the truth heareth my voice,' said Christ. And in his first epistle St John declared: 'He that knoweth God heareth us; he that is not of God heareth not us.' May we not approach the writings of Staretz Silouan in the light of these words?

Though the Staretz was almost unlettered, his notes, which were an attempt to record what was revealed to him, both in content and form, often read like the Psalms. This is natural, since they were born of unceasing prayer. The beat is slow, the typical rhythm of prayer in the deep heart. Again and again he returns to the same themes, few in number but so ontologically profound that they present us with the final criterion - God and all things heavenly can be known only through the Holy Spirit; the Lord has an immense love for man which we may know in the Holy Spirit; the Holy Spirit is the spirit of humility, peace and integrity; the Holy Spirit is the spirit of compassion and love for enemies. To live impregnated to the depths of one's being with these ideas is to have a secret spiritual prism through which to contemplate the whole world.

The Staretz was a man of a single vision, inspired by God's searchless manifestation to him, which irradiated his whole being. When the Lord was thus manifest to him, he saw that God was infinite love, universal love. The Holy Spirit revealed to him the Divinity of Christ. The Holy Spirit taught him humility and an all-embracing love for every created being. And day and night he sought to re-live his experience of divine eternity.

Repeated visitations by the Holy Spirit and long years of titanic spiritual struggle, led to a form of dogmatic consciousness.

And when he received from on High intimations of the ways of God he felt bound to share the glad tidings of salvation in Christ. He was a man of few words but this perhaps betokens their truth. The little he said can penetrate to the heart and regenerate the soul. He was a man of few words but there is a very great deal to be said about him and his utterances if we would uncover their theological content, which often passes unrecognised.* As a general rule, verbosity suggests deviation in one form or other from divine truth. But if we would concentrate on divine truth as seen in Christ, all need for a stream of words disappears, until finally the mind enters the realm of profound silence.

To read the Staretz, to follow his train of thought, analyse his heart, study the way he expresses himself, is to realise that he learned not from people, not from books, but directly from the Spirit of God. This is why his teaching is in such keeping with Christ's commandments. There is no trace of any sickly exaltation, no indulgence in rhetoric - even when he addresses himself 'to all the people of the earth', for whom he prayed year after year.

The Staretz was, as it were, possessed by his vision of the Divinity of Christ, by the 'sweetness' of the Holy Spirit. And he implemented this vision in his life. The Holy Spirit did, in truth, make him like unto Christ Himself, Whom it was vouchsafed to him to see and of Whose likeness he so often talked, quoting the great apostle of love, 'We shall be like him; for we shall see him as he is'.

The Staretz' whole life bore witness, first and foremost, to the principle that love for enemies is a true sign of the grace of the Holy Spirit. He roundly declared that where there is no love for enemies, there can be no proper knowledge of God. Where hate operates, he saw - despite all prophetic pathos and even claim to be doing God service (cf. John xvi, 2) - the face of the black abyss.

---

*It may be noted in this connection that Christ's comparatively rare words, which offer no direct indication of any wealth of theology, have given birth down the centuries, and continue to give birth, to great theological schools. *17*

The testimony of a man like Staretz Silouan, totally innocent of intellectual wiles; the witness of one who throughout his whole life spilled his heart's blood in prayer for the entire world, must have especial force and meaning.

It seems to me that the Staretz was as receptive and spontaneous as the first apostles. The fact that he remained untouched by the falsities of our contemporary civilisation makes him irresistibly convincing. So then, those who were not acquainted with him personally can judge of him by his writings, while those who knew him and saw his genuine simplicity and humility are persuaded that here was a man of God.

Staretz Silouan 'kept his mind in hell, and despaired not'. He battled against the 'great and strong wind, the earthquake and fire' of temptation. And now he speaks to us in the still small voice of the Lord.

1

Of the Knowledge of God

THE Father so loved us that He gave us His Son; but such was the will of the Son too, and He became incarnate and lived with us on earth. And the holy Apostles and a multitude of people beheld the Lord in the flesh, but not all knew Him as the Lord; yet it has been given to me, a poor sinner, through the Holy Spirit to know that Jesus Christ is God.

The Lord loves man and reveals Himself to man. And when the soul beholds the Lord she humbly rejoices in the Master's compassion, and from that hour her love for her Creator is greater than her any other love: though she may see all things and love all men, yet will she love the Lord above all.

The soul suddenly sees the Lord and knows that it is He.

Who shall describe this joy, this gladness?

The Lord is made known in the Holy Spirit, and the Holy Spirit pervades the *entire* man—soul, mind and body.

After this wise is God known in heaven and on earth.

The Lord in His boundless mercy granted this grace to me, a sinner, that others might come to know God and turn to Him.

I write out of the grace of God.

Yea, this is truth.

The Lord Himself is my Witness.

The Merciful Lord gave the Holy Spirit on earth, and by the Holy Spirit was the Holy Church established.

The Holy Spirit unfolded to us not only the things of the earth but those too which are of heaven.

The Prophets, the beloved of the Lord, rejoiced in the Holy Spirit, wherefore the words that they spake were mighty and pleasant, for every soul would hear the word of the Lord.

Filled with love the holy Apostles went into all the world, preaching salvation to mankind and fearing nothing, for the Spirit of God was their strength. When St Andrew was threatened with death upon the cross if he did not stay his preaching he answered:

'If I feared the cross I should not be preaching the Cross.'

In this manner all the other Apostles, and after them the martyrs and holy men who wrestled against evil, went forward with joy to meet pain and suffering. For the Holy Spirit, sweet and gracious, draws the soul to love the Lord, and in the sweetness of the Holy Spirit the soul loses her fear of suffering.

The Lord is love; and He commanded us to love one another and to love our enemies; and the Holy Spirit teaches us this love.

The soul that has not come to know the Holy Spirit does not understand how it is possible to love one's enemies, and will not receive this commandment; but in the Lord is pity for all men, and he who would be with the Lord must love his enemies.

How may we know whether the Lord loves us or no?

Here are tokens: If you battle firmly against sin the Lord loves you. If you love your enemies you are even more beloved of God. And if you lay down your life for others you are greatly beloved of the Lord, who Himself laid down His life for us.

The man who has known the Lord through the Holy Spirit becomes like unto the Lord, as St John the Divine said: 'We shall be like him; for we shall see him as he is.' And we shall behold his glory.

Many numbers of people, you say, are suffering every kind of adversity and from evil men. But I entreat you: Humble yourself beneath the strong hand of God, and grace will be your teacher and you yourself will long to suffer for the sake of the love of the

Lord. That is what the Holy Spirit, whom we have come to know in the Church, will teach you.

But the man who cries out against evil men, who does not pray for them will never know the grace of God.

If you would know of the Lord's love for us, hate sin and wrong thoughts, and day and night pray fervently. The Lord will then give you His grace, and you will know Him through the Holy Spirit, and after death, when you enter into paradise, there too you will know the Lord through the Holy Spirit, as you knew Him on earth.

We do not need riches or learning in order to know the Lord: we must simply be obedient and sober, have a humble spirit and love our fellow-men. The Lord will love a soul that does this, and of His own accord make Himself manifest to her and instruct her in love and humility, and give her all things necessary for her to find rest in God.

We may study as much as we will but we shall still not come to know the Lord unless we live according to His commandments, for the Lord is not made known through learning but by the Holy Spirit. Many philosophers and scholars have arrived at a belief in the existence of God, but they have not come to know God.

To believe in a God is one thing, to know God another.

Both in heaven and on earth the Lord is made known only by the Holy Spirit, and not through ordinary learning. Even children, who have no learning at all, come to know the Lord by the Holy Spirit. St John the Baptist felt the presence of the Lord while still in his mother's womb. St Simeon Stylites was a seven-year-old boy when the Lord appeared to him and he knew Him; St Seraphim a grown man of twenty-seven when the Lord showed Himself to him during the Liturgy; and another Simeon was stricken with years when he received the Lord in his arms in the temple, and knew Him.

Some there are who spend their whole lives in trying to find out about the sun, or the moon, or in seeking like knowledge;

yet this is of no profit to the soul. But if we take pains to explore the human heart this is what we shall see: the kingdom of heaven in the soul of the saint, but in the soul of the sinner are darkness and torment. And it is good to know this because we shall dwell eternally either in the kingdom or in torment.

Just as the love of Jesus Christ is beyond our understanding so we cannot conceive of the depth of His suffering, because our own love for the Lord is so infinitely small. But with greater love comes more understanding even of the Lord's sufferings. There is love in small degree, medium love and perfect love; and the more perfect our love the more perfect our knowledge.

We are able to treat of God only in so far as we have known the grace of the Holy Spirit; for how can a man think on and consider a thing that he has not seen or heard tell of, and does not know? Now the Saints declare that they have seen God; yet there are people who say that God is not. No doubt they say this inasmuch as they have not known God, but it does not at all mean that He is not.

The Saints speak of that which they have actually seen, of that which they know. They do not speak of something they have not seen. (They do not tell us, for instance, that they have seen a horse a mile long or a steamer ten miles long, which do not exist.) And I think that, if God were not, there would be no intimation of Him on earth; but people want to live after their own fashion and consequently they declare that God is not, and in so doing they establish that He is.

Even the souls of the heathen sensed that God is, though they were ignorant how to worship the true God. But the Holy Spirit instructed the Prophets of old and after them the Apostles and then our holy Fathers and bishops, and in this wise the true faith came down to us. And we knew the Lord by the Holy Spirit, and when we knew Him our souls were confirmed in Him.

The Lord loves us so dearly that it passes description. Through the Holy Spirit alone can the soul know His love, of which she is inexpressibly aware. The Lord is all goodness and mercy. He is meek and gentle, and we have no words to tell of His goodness; but the soul without words feels this love and would remain wrapped in its quiet tranquillity for ever.

Christ said: 'I will not leave you comfortless', and we see, in truth, that He did not forsake us but gave us the Holy Spirit.

O ye peoples of the earth, fashioned by God, know your Creator and His love for us! Know the love of Christ, and live in peace and thereby rejoice the Lord, who in His mercy waits for all men to come unto Him.

Turn to Him, all ye peoples of the earth, and lift your prayers to God. And the prayers of the whole earth shall rise to heaven like a soft and lovely cloud lit by the sun, and all the heavens will rejoice and sing praises to the Lord for His sufferings whereby He saved us.

Know, all ye peoples, that we are created for the glory of God in the heavens. Cleave not to the earth, for God is our Father and He loves us like beloved children.

O Lord grant to all nations to know Thee by Thy Holy Spirit. As Thou didst give the Holy Spirit to the Apostles and they knew Thee, so grant to all men to know Thee by Thy Holy Spirit.

2

On Love

MY soul thirsts for the living God. Time and again my soul seeks fulness of delight in the Lord. O mercy of God that passeth all understanding: the Lord formed man of the dust of the ground, and breathed into his nostrils the breath of life, and the soul of man was made kin to God.

The Lord so loved His creature that He gave man the Holy Spirit, and man knew his Creator and loved his Lord.

The Holy Spirit is love and sweetness to the soul, the mind and the body; but when the soul loses grace, or grace is diminished, once again the soul will seek the Holy Spirit in tears, and yearn for God and cry:

My soul yearns for the Lord, and I seek Him in tears.

How could I not seek Thee, O Lord? For Thou Thyself didst seek me out aforehand, and gavest me to delight in Thy Holy Spirit; and now my soul yearns for Thee. My heart fell to loving Thee, and I pray Thee: give me to the end to abide in Thy love. For the sake of Thy love empower me to endure all sickness and affliction.

My soul is seized with fear and trembling when I would write of the love of God.

My soul is poor and without strength to describe the Lord's love.

My spirit fails, but love constrains me to write.

The Lord ascended into heaven and awaits our coming; but to be with the Lord we must be like Him, or like little children —lowly and meek—and we must serve Him. Then, according to the words of the Lord, 'Where I am, there shall also my servant be', we too shall be with Him in the kingdom of heaven. But now my soul is overspread with melancholy, and I am unable to lift an undistracted mind to God, and I have no tears wherewith to bewail my evil deeds: my soul is withered away and spent with the night of this life.

O who shall sing me the song that I have loved since the days of my youth—the song of the Lord's Ascension into heaven, of His love for us, of the vigil He keeps for our coming? To this song would I hearken with tears, for my soul is weary on earth.

What has befallen me? How came I to lose joy, and shall I attain to joy again?

Weep with me, all ye wild beasts and birds. Weep with me, forest and desert. Weep with me, every creature created of God, and comfort me in my grief and sorrow.

O man, what a feeble creature thou art.

When grace dwells within us the spirit glows and reaches day and night towards the Lord, for grace constrains the soul to love God; and now that she has come to love Him she cannot tear herself away from Him: never can she have enough of the tenderness of the Holy Spirit.

And there is no end to the love of God.

I know a man whom the Lord in His mercy visited with His grace. And had the Lord asked him, 'Wouldst thou have Me give thee more?', from the weakness of the flesh his soul would have made answer: 'Thou seest, Lord, that I cannot bear more but would die.' For man has little strength and may not carry the fulness of grace.

Thus it was that on Mount Tabor the Disciples fell on their face before the glory of the Lord.

With what shall I requite my Lord?

At all times I beseech the Lord who is merciful to grant that I may love my enemies; and by the grace of God I have experienced what the love of God is, and what it is to love my neighbour; and day and night I pray the Lord for love, and the Lord gives me tears to weep for the whole world. But if I find fault with any man or look on him with an unkind eye my tears dry up and my soul sinks into despondency. Yet do I begin again to entreat forgiveness of the Lord, and the Lord in His mercy forgives me, a sinner.

Brethren, before the face of my God I write: Humble your hearts, and while yet on this earth look upon the mercy of the Lord.

No man of himself can know what is God's love, unless he be taught of the Holy Spirit; but God's love is known in our Church through the Holy Spirit, and so we speak of this love.

The sinful soul which does not know the Lord fears death, thinking that the Lord will not forgive her her sins. But this is because the soul does not know the Lord and how greatly He loves us. But if people knew this, then no man would despair in his heart, for the Lord not only forgives but rejoices exceedingly at the return of a sinner. Though you be at death's door believe firmly that the moment you ask you will receive forgiveness.

The Lord is not like us. He is passing meek, and merciful, and good; and when the soul knows Him she marvels greatly and exclaims: 'O what a Lord is ours!'

The Holy Spirit gave our Church to know how great is God's mercy.

The Lord loves us, and gently and without reproach takes us to Himself, just as the father in the Gospel story did not reproach his prodigal son but called his servants to bring a new robe and put a precious ring on his finger and shoes on his feet, and told them to kill the fatted calf, and be merry; and in nothing did he condemn his son.

'Did not our heart burn within us?' said the Apostles after Christ drew near them. So does the soul recognize and love her Lord, and the delight of His love is a burning delight.

In heaven there is one and the same love in the hearts of all, but on earth some there are that greatly love the Lord, others love Him in small degree, while still others love Him not at all.

The soul that is filled with love of God is forgetful both of heaven and earth. The spirit burns and invisibly beholds the Desired One, and the soul sheds many sweet tears and is unable to forget the Lord for a single second, for the grace of God gives strength to love the Beloved.

Brethren, let us humble ourselves that we may be worthy of the love of God, that the Lord may adorn us with His lowliness of spirit and His humility, that we may become worthy of the heavenly mansions which the Lord has made ready for us.

The Lord loves all men but His love is greater for the man who seeks Him.

'I love them that love me,' said the Lord. 'And those that seek me shall find grace.' And with grace life is good, and the soul rejoices and says: 'My Lord—I am THY servant.'

In these words there is great joy: if the Lord is *ours, then all things are ours.* That is how rich we are.

Great and inapprehensible is our Lord, but for our sakes He made Himself small that we might know Him and love Him, that for love of Him we might forget the earth, and live in heaven and behold the glory of the Lord.

The Lord bestows such grace on His chosen that they embrace the whole earth, the whole world, with their love, and their souls burn with longing that all men should be saved and behold the glory of the Lord.

The Lord said to His holy Disciples: 'Children, have ye any meat?' What great love is expressed in those tender words! The Lord calls us 'Children'! What could rejoice us more? We should ponder these words and think on the Lord's sufferings for us on the Cross.

On earth the soul has only to touch upon the love of God for the sweetness of the Holy Spirit to transport her with wonder at her beloved God and Heavenly Father.

O how the Lord loves His creation!

And behold the Lord has vouchsafed to us to speak together of these things, and our spirit rejoices that the Lord is with us.

Humbly I entreat you—pray for me, and the Lord will reward you.

Brother R. told me how once when he lay seriously ill his mother said to his father: 'How ill our little lad is! I would gladly let myself be cut in pieces if it would help him and ease his suffering.'

The Lord's love for man is like that. He said: 'Greater love hath no man than this, that a man lay down his life for his fellow.' The Lord's compassion for us was so strong that He wanted to suffer for us, as a mother suffers, and even more. But no man can conceive of this great love without the grace of the Holy Spirit. The Scriptures tell of this love but neither are they to be understood by the mind, for in the Scriptures too speaks the same Holy Spirit.

The love of the Lord is such that He would have all men saved: His desire is that all should abide eternally with Him in heaven, and behold His glory. We do not know the fulness of this glory, but through the Holy Spirit we may conceive of it in part. But the man who has not come to know the Holy Spirit can have no conception of this glory: he can only believe in the promise of the Lord, and keep His commandments. However, he too is blessed, as the Lord showed St Thomas, and will have equal place with those who saw the glory of God while still here on earth.

If you would know the Lord, humble yourself to the utmost. Be obedient and sober in all things. Love truth. And the Lord *of a surety* will give you to know Him through the Holy Spirit; and then you will know by experience what love towards God is, and what love towards man. And the more perfect the love, the more perfect your knowledge. There is love in small measure; there is a mean of love; and there is great love.

The man who fears sin loves God. The man with a tender heart loves Him more. Still greater is the love of the man in whose soul dwell light and joy. But the man with grace in soul and body has perfect love. This is the grace the Holy Spirit gave to the Martyrs, the grace that helped them to bear every suffering with fortitude.

I would speak for a moment (insomuch as the grace of God will enlighten me) of the various degrees of love for God.

Where a man fears to distress God by sinning in any way—that is the first degree of love. The man whose mind is undistracted has love in the second degree, which is greater than the first. A third and still greater degree of love is when a man is aware of grace in his soul. And, finally, the man who has the grace of the Holy Spirit both in soul and body is in a state of perfect love; and if he preserve this grace the bones of his body will turn into sacred relics, as did the bones of the holy Martyrs, the Prophets, the blessed Fathers, and other great Saints.

We are proud-minded, and therefore unable to continue in this grace, which withdraws from the soul. Then the soul yearns after the grace she has lost, and seeks it anew with tears, and weeps and sobs and calls upon the Lord, saying:

'O merciful Lord, Thou seest my soul's mourning, and how I long for Thee.'

There is no man on earth so gentle and lowly in spirit as our Lord Jesus Christ. In Him is our joy, in Him our gladness. Let us give Him our love, and He will lead us into His kingdom, where we shall behold His glory.

These forty years, ever since the Lord through the Holy Spirit gave me to know the love of God, have I grieved over God's people.

O brethren, there is naught better than the love of God when the Lord fires the soul with love for God and our fellow-man.

The man who knows the delight of the love of God—when the soul, warmed by grace, loves both God and her brother—knows in part that 'the kingdom of God is within us'.

Blessed is the soul that loves her brother, for *our brother is our life*.

Blessed is the soul that loves her brother. The Spirit of the Lord lives manifest within her, giving peace and gladness, and she weeps for the whole world.

My soul has remembered the Lord's love, and my heart is grown warm. My soul is given over to bitter weeping that I have so deeply grieved the Lord, my beloved Creator; but He remembered not my sins; and then my soul surrendered to profound and sorrowful weeping that the Lord might have mercy on every soul and take each one into His heavenly kingdom.

And my soul weeps for the whole world.

I cannot remain silent concerning the people, whom I love so greatly that I must weep for them. I cannot remain silent because my soul ever grieves for the people of God, and I pray for them with tears. I cannot refrain from making known to you, brethren, the mercy of God and the wiles of the enemy.

Forty years have gone by since the grace of the Holy Spirit taught me to love mankind and every created thing, and revealed unto me the wiles of the enemy, who works his evil in the world by means of deceit.

Love does not depend on time, and the power of love continues always. There are some who believe that the Lord suffered death for love of man but because they do not attain to this love in their own souls it seems to them that it is an old story of bygone days. But when the soul knows the love of God by the Holy Spirit she feels without a shadow of doubt that the Lord is our Father, the closest, the best and dearest of fathers, and there is no greater happiness than to love God with all our hearts, with all our souls and with all our minds, according to the Lord's commandment, and our neighbour as ourself. And when this love is in the soul, everything rejoices her; but when it is lost sight of man cannot find peace, and is troubled, and blames others as if they had done him an injury, and does not realise that he himself is at fault—he has lost his love for God and has accused or conceived a hatred for his brother.

Grace proceeds from brotherly love, and by brotherly love is grace preserved; but if we do not love our brother the grace of God will not come into our souls.

If people kept Christ's commandments there would be paradise on earth, and with little labour every man would suffice his needs, and the Spirit of God would live in the souls of men, for He Himself seeks us and would dwell in us, and if He does not take up His abode in us it is only because of the proudness of our minds.

Men's hearts have grown proud, and it is only through affliction and repentance that we arrive at salvation, while as for love— it is rarely attained.

If a man thinks kindly of his brother, deeming that the Lord loves him—and especially if he believes that the Holy Spirit dwells in his soul—that man is near to the love of God.

One of you may object: this discourse is all of the love of God. But what else should we deliberate on but God? Did He not create us that we might live eternally with Him and behold His glory? When a man loves, his desire is to talk of the object of his love; and then habit enters in. If you make it a habit to think of God, you will always carry God with you in your soul. If you are always thinking of worldly things, they will absorb your mind. Make a habit of meditating on the Lord's sufferings, or on eternal fire, and they will become part of your soul.

God helps us in what is good, while the enemy incites us to evil, but this depends also on our own wills: we must constrain ourselves to what is good, but with moderation and knowing the measure of our strength. We must study our souls to know what is salutary for us: it may be more profitable to one man to pray, for another to read or write. It is a good thing to read but it is better to pray without distraction, and better still to weep: to each as it is given to him by the Lord. To be sure, when we rise from sleep we must render thanks to God, then repent and pray our fill. Next, we should read to rest the mind, and after that pray again, and work. Grace proceeds from everything that is good, but above all from brotherly love.

The soul should be filled with such insatiable love of God that the mind in all its strength dwells continually in God, captive only to Him.

The man who has come to loathe sin has mounted the first rung of the heavenly ladder. When he is not tempted in his heart to sin his foot is already on the second rung; while the man who through the Holy Spirit has come to know perfect love of God has reached the third step of the ladder. But this rarely happens.

If we wish to love God we must observe all that the Lord commanded us in the Gospels. Our hearts must brim with compassion and not only feel love for our fellow-men but pity for every creature—for every thing created of God.

That green leaf on the tree which you needlessly plucked: it was not wrong, only rather a pity for the little leaf. The heart that has learned to love feels sorry for every created thing. But man is a supreme creation, and therefore if you see that he has gone astray and is bringing destruction on himself pray for him and weep for him if you are able, or at least sigh before God for him. And the soul that acts after this fashion is loved of the Lord, for she is like unto him.

If you think evil of people, it means you have an evil spirit in you whispering evil thoughts about others. And if a man dies without repenting, without having forgiven his brother, his soul will go to the place where lives the evil spirit which possessed his soul.

This is the law we have: if you forgive others, it is a sign that the Lord has forgiven you. But if you refuse to forgive, then your own sin remains with you.

The Lord wants us to love our fellow-man; and if you reflect that the Lord loves him, that is a sign of the Lord's love in you. And if you consider how greatly the Lord loves His creature, and you yourself have compassion on all creation, and love your enemies, counting yourself the vilest of men, this is a sign of abundant grace of the Holy Spirit in you.

The man who has the Holy Spirit within him, in however slight a degree, sorrows day and night for all mankind. His heart is filled with pity for all God's creatures, and more especially for those who do not know God or who resist Him and therefore are bound for the fire of torment. For them, more than for himself, he prays night and day, that all may repent and know the Lord.

Christ prayed for those who were crucifying Him: 'Father, forgive them; for they know not what they do.' St Stephen prayed for those who stoned him, that the Lord 'lay not this sin to their charge'. And we, if we wish to preserve grace, must pray for our enemies. If you do not feel pity for the sinner destined to suffer the pains of fire, it means that the grace of the Holy Spirit is not in you, but an evil spirit lives in you. While you are still alive, therefore, strive by repentance to free yourself from this spirit.

The Lord taught me to love my enemies. Without the grace of God we cannot love our enemies, but the Holy Spirit teaches love, and then even devils rouse our pity because they have fallen from good, and lost humility and love of God.

I beseech you, put this to the test. When a man affronts you or brings dishonour on your head, or takes what is yours, or persecutes the Church, pray to the Lord, and say: 'O Lord, we are all

Thy creatures. Have pity on Thy servants, and turn their hearts to repentance,' and you will be aware of grace in your soul. To begin with, constrain your heart to love her enemies, and the Lord, seeing your good will, will help you in all things, and experience itself will show you the way. But the man who thinks with malice of his enemies has not God's love within him and does not know God.

If you will pray for your enemies, peace will come to you; but when you come to love your enemies—know that a great measure of the grace of God dwells in you, though I do not say perfect grace as yet, but sufficient for salvation. Whereas if you revile your enemies it means there is an evil spirit living in you and bringing evil thoughts into your heart, for, in the words of the Lord, out of the heart proceed evil thoughts or good thoughts.

If you cannot love, then at least do not revile and curse your enemies, and things will already be better; but if a man curse and abuse his enemies it is plain that an evil spirit abides in him, and when he dies he will go to the abode of evil spirits. May the Lord preserve every soul from such adversity!

Understand me. It is so simple. People who do not know God, or who go against Him, are to be pitied: the heart sorrows for them and the eye weeps. Both paradise and torment are clearly visible to us: we know them through the Holy Spirit. And did not the Lord Himself say: 'The kingdom of God is within you'? Thus eternal life has its beginnings here in this life; and here it is that we sow the seeds of eternal torment.

Where there is pride there cannot be grace, and if we lose grace we also lose both love of God and assurance in prayer. The soul is then tormented by evil thoughts and does not understand that she must humble herself and love her enemies, for there is no other way to please God.

'The enemy persecutes our Holy Church,' you may say. 'Am I then to love him?' But my answer is this: 'Your poor soul has not come to know God, and how greatly He loves us, and how longingly He looks for all men to repent and be saved.' The Lord is love, and He sent the Holy Spirit on earth, Who teaches the soul to love her enemies and pray for them that they too may find salvation. That is true love. But if they are judged according to their deeds, then they merit punishment.

Glory be to the Lord for His great love towards us, that He forgives us our sins and reveals His mysteries to us by the Holy Spirit!

The Lord gave us the commandment 'Love your enemies'. But how are we to love them when they do us evil? Or how can we love those who persecute the Holy Church?

When the Lord was on His way to Jerusalem and the Samaritans did not receive Him, His disciples John and James were ready to call down fire from heaven to consume them; but the Lord in His mercy said: 'I am not come to destroy but to save'. Thus should we have but one thought: that all should be saved. The soul sorrows for her enemies and prays for them because they have strayed from the truth and their faces are set towards hell. That is love for our enemies. When Judas bethought him to betray the Lord, the Lord was stirred to pity and showed him what he was doing. Thus must we too be gentle with those who err and stray, and we shall be saved by God's mercy.

Love is made known through the Holy Spirit. And the Holy Spirit the soul knows through peace and the sweet savour of the Lord. O how we should render thanks to God for His great love towards us! Consider, my beloved brethren: the Lord bestows His Holy Spirit on the sinful soul and gives her to know His mercy. And to know God we have no need of riches: we need only love our neighbour and be lowly in spirit, sober and obedient, and for these virtues the Lord allows us to know Him. Could any thing in the world be more precious than this knowledge? To know God, to know how He loves us and enlightens our spirits in the way they should go?

Where would you find a father prepared to die on the cross for the transgressions of his children? The ordinary father grieves and is sorry for his son who must be punished for his wrong-doing; but for all his pity he tells him that he has done wrong and that it is right that he should be punished for his crimes.

But the Lord will never say this to us. He will ask us, too, as he asked the apostle Peter: 'Lovest thou me?' Thus in paradise He will say to the whole people: 'And you—do you love Me?' And all will answer Him: 'Yea, Lord, we love Thee. Thou didst save us by Thy sufferings on the Cross, and now Thou hast given us the gift of the Kingdom of Heaven'.

And no man shall be ashamed in heaven, as Adam and Eve were ashamed after the fall; but meekness, love and humility shall reign—not the humility we know now when we humble ourselves and bear with obloquy or reckon ourselves the worst of men, but all shall have Christ-like humility which is beyond the comprehension of every one, save of those who have been taught of the Holy Spirit.

What shall I render Thee, O Lord, for that Thou hast poured such great mercy on my soul? Grant, I beg Thee, that I may see my iniquities and ever weep before Thee, for Thou art filled with love for humble souls and dost give them the grace of the Holy Spirit.

O merciful God, forgive me. Thou seest how my soul is drawn to Thee, her Creator. Thou hast wounded my soul with Thy love, and she thirsts for Thee, and wearies without end, and day and night, insatiable, reaches towards Thee, and has no wish to look upon this world, though I love the earth, but above all I love Thee, my Creator, and my soul longs for Thee.

O my Creator, why have I, Thy little creature, grieved Thee so often? Yet hast Thou not remembered my sins.

3

The Soul's Yearning for God

MY soul yearns after the Lord.

How could I not seek Thee? For Thou first didst seek me. Thou gavest me to delight in Thy Holy Spirit, and my soul rejoices that Thou art my God and my Lord.

In the first year of my life in the monastery my soul apprehended God in the Holy Spirit.

The Lord loves us greatly: this I know by the Holy Spirit Whom the Lord gave me in His singular mercy.

I am an old man, preparing for death, and I write of truth for the sake of the people.

The Spirit of Christ Whom I had of the Lord desires the salvation of all, that all should know God.

The Lord gave the thief paradise; thus will He give paradise to every sinner. I with my sins am odious and unclean but I turned to God for forgiveness, and He granted me *not forgiveness alone but the Holy Spirit,* and in the Holy Spirit I knew God.

Do you see God's love for us? And who shall describe His mercy?

O my brethren, on my knees I beg you to believe in God-- believe that there is a Holy Spirit Who bears witness to Him in every church, and in my soul.

The Holy Spirit is love; and the souls of all the holy who dwell in heaven overflow with this love. And on earth this same Holy Spirit is in the souls of those who love God.

All heaven beholds the earth in the Holy Spirit, and hears our prayers and carries them to God.

My soul knows that the Lord is merciful, but His mercy passes portrayal. He is exceeding meek and lowly, and when the soul perceives Him she is all transformed into love towards God and her neighbour, and becomes meek and lowly herself. But if a man lose grace, he will weep like Adam driven from paradise. Adam wept and the whole desert heard his sobbing; his tears were bitter with affliction and he wept them for many years.

In such wise the soul who has known and lost the grace of God yearns for God and cries:

'My soul yearns after God, and I seek Him in tears.'

The grace of God gives strength to love the Beloved; and the soul is drawn to pray unceasingly and cannot even for a moment forget the Lord.

My soul languishes on earth and longs for the things of heaven.

The Lord came down to earth to raise us to where He Himself dwells with His most holy Mother, who served Him on earth for the sake of our salvation, and with all the Disciples and followers of the Lord.

The Lord calls us thither, in spite of our sins.

There shall we behold the holy Apostles in glory for their preaching of the Gospel; there shall we see saintly monks who wrestled in fasting to humble their souls; there those who assumed folly for Christ's sake are glorified because they overcame the world. There all those who have conquered themselves will be glorified, and all those who prayed for the world and bore the burden of the whole world's sorrows because theirs was the love of Christ, and love cannot suffer a single soul to perish.

It is there that the soul would take up her abode; but nothing unclean shall enter where those who come in arrive by way of great tribulations and chastening of spirit and many tears; and only children, who have not lost the grace of holy baptism, enter therein without affliction, and there in the Holy Spirit they know the Lord.

My soul yearns after God and prays day and night, for the Name of the Lord is sweet and dear to the prayerful soul, and warms the soul to love God.

We live a long time on this earth and we love the beauty of the earth: the sky and the sun, gardens, sea and river, forest and meadow, music too, and all the beauties of the world. But when the soul comes to know our Lord Jesus Christ she has no further desire for the things of the earth.

Wondrous are the works of the Lord: out of the dust of the ground He created man, and gave this creature of dust to know Him in the Holy Spirit, so that man says, 'My Lord and my God'; and these words he utters from the fulness of faith and love.

What more could the soul seek on earth?

Here is a great miracle: the soul *on a sudden* knows her Creator and His love.

When the soul sees the Lord, how meek and humble He is, then she herself is *thoroughly* humbled, and desires nothing so much as the humility of Christ. And however long the soul may live on earth, she will always desire and seek this humility which passes comprehension, which she cannot forget.

If the Lord has left us ignorant of the ordering of many things in this world, then it means it is not necessary for us to know: we cannot compass all creation with our minds.

But the Creator Himself of heaven and earth and every created thing gives us to know Him in the Holy Spirit. In this same Holy Spirit we know the Mother of God, the Angels and Saints, and our spirit burns with love for them.

But he who will not love his enemies cannot come to know the Lord and the sweetness of the Holy Spirit. The Holy Spirit teaches us to love our enemies, so that the soul pities them as if they were her own children.

There are people who desire the destruction, the torment in hell-fire, of their enemies, or of the enemies of the Church. They think like that because they have not learnt from the Holy Spirit the love of God, for he who has learnt the love of God will shed tears for the whole world.

You say that So-and-so is an evil-doer, and may he burn in hell-fire.

But I would ask you: supposing God were to give you a fair place in paradise and you saw burning in the fire the man to whom you had wished the tortures of hell—would you really even then not feel pity for him, whoever he might be, even an enemy of the Church?

Or is it that you have a heart of iron? But there is no place for iron in paradise. Paradise has need of humility and the love of Christ, which pities all men.

The grace of God is not in the man who does not love his enemies.

It is given to our Orthodox Church through the Holy Spirit to understand the mysteries of God, and she is strong in the holiness of her thought and in her patience.

The Orthodox soul is taught by grace to hold fast to the Lord and His most holy Mother, and our spirit rejoices in the contemplation of God Whom we know.

But we can only know God by the Holy Spirit, and the proud man who aspires to know the Creator with his intelligence is blind and stupid.

With our minds we cannot come to know even how the sun was made; and if we beg God to tell us how He made the sun the answer rings clear in our soul: 'Humble thyself and thou shalt know not only the sun but the Creator of the sun.'

But when the soul comes to know the Lord for very joy she forgets the sun and every created thing, and abandons all anxiety for earthly knowledge.

The Lord gave us the Holy Spirit, and we learnt the song of the Lord, and so we forget the earth for sweetness of the love of God.

The Lord's love is an ardent love and allows no thought of the earth. He who has experienced this love seeks it tirelessly day and night and is drawn towards it. But this love is lost to us with the approach of pride and conceit, enmity, fault-finding and envy. This love forsakes us because of an incontinent thought, or attachment to earthly things. In face of these grace departs, and the soul, desolate and despondent, then yearns for God, as our father Adam yearned after his exile from paradise.

If we understood the force of Christ's words, 'Learn humility and meekness of me', the whole world, the whole universe would abandon all other knowledge to study this heavenly science.

Men are ignorant of the power of Christ's humility, and that is why they aspire to the things of this earth; but without the Holy Spirit they cannot know the force of these words of Christ. But he who has learned to know will never forsake his knowledge, even were he offered all the kingdoms of the world.

Life is burdensome without love towards God, the soul feels sombre and stale; but with the coming of love the soul's joy passes description.

My soul thirsts after the humility of Christ, and yearns for it day and night, and at times I cry with a loud cry:

'My soul yearns for Thee, O Lord, and weeping I seek Thee.'

My brethren, I weep as I write these lines.

When the soul comes to know the Lord by the Holy Spirit, she stands in everlasting wonder before God's compassion, His majesty and might. But if the soul has not yet learned but is only learning humility, she will be subject to alternating states: now contending with intrusive thoughts which give her no rest, now freed from such thoughts and able to contemplate the Lord and perceive His love. Wherefore the Lord saith:

'Learn of me, for I am meek and lowly in heart; and ye shall find rest unto your souls.'

And if a man will not learn humility, love and goodness, the Lord will not let that man know Him. But the soul that has come to know the Lord in the Holy Spirit is pierced by His love and cannot forget Him; just as a sick man is ever mindful of his sickness, so the soul that loves the Lord is always mindful of the Lord and of His love for all mankind.

Blessed is the soul that knows her Creator and has grown to love Him, for she has found perfect rest in Him.

The Lord is merciful beyond bounds.

My soul knows His mercy towards me, and I write of it in hope that even one soul may come to love the Lord and be turned to Him by the fire of repentance.

If the Lord had not given me to know His mercy in the Holy Spirit, I should have despaired by reason of the multitude of my sins, but He enraptured my soul, and my soul loved Him and forgets all that is of the earth.

O Lord, humble my heart that I may be ever pleasing to Thee.

The Lord bids us love Him with all our hearts and all our souls —but how is it possible to love Him Whom we have never seen, and how may we learn this love? The Lord is made known by His effect on the soul. When the Lord has visited her, the soul knows that a dear Guest has come and gone, and she yearns for Him and seeks Him with tears: 'Where art Thou, my Light, where art Thou, my Joy? Thy trace is fragrant in my soul but Thou art not there and my soul yearns for Thee, and my heart aches and is sad, and nothing rejoices me because I have grieved my Lord and He hath hidden Himself from my sight.

Were we like simple children, the Lord would show us His paradise and we should see Him in the glory of the Cherubim and Seraphim, and of all the heavenly host and the Saints; but we are not humble and therefore we torment ourselves and those we live among.

What joy is ours that the Lord not only forgives our sins but allows the soul to know Him, so soon as she humbles herself. The poorest wretch may humble himself and know God in the Holy Spirit. There is no need of money or of possessions to know God, only of humility. The Lord freely gives Himself, for His mercy's sake alone. I did not know this before, but now every day and hour, every minute, I clearly see the mercy of God. The Lord gives peace even in sleep, but without God there is no peace in the soul.

The Lord does not reveal Himself to many because of their intellectual pride; yet they think that they have much knowledge. But what is their knowledge worth, if they know not the Lord, know not the grace of the Holy Spirit, know not how this grace comes and wherefore it is lost?

But let us humble ourselves, brethren, and the Lord will show us all things, as a loving father shows all things to his children.

Some there are who argue about faith, and there is no end to such disputes. We must not quarrel about faith but only pray to God and His Mother, and the Lord will enlighten us (not by means of argument), and will enlighten us speedily.

Many men have made a study of all the faiths, but the true faith they have not come to know as they should; but if a man will pray to God in humility that the Lord may enlighten him, the Lord will make known to him how greatly He loves mankind.

The proud man thinks he can comprehend everything with his mind. The Lord does not grant this.

We know the Lord: He has made Himself manifest to us in the Holy Spirit, and the soul knows Him, and is joyful and glad and at ease, and in this lies our holy life.

The Lord said: 'Where I am, there shall also my servant be, and he shall see my glory.' But we do not understand the Scriptures. Now when the Holy Spirit teaches, everything becomes comprehensible and the soul feels as if she were in heaven, for the same Holy Spirit is in heaven and on earth, in the Holy Scriptures, and in the souls of those who love God. Without the Holy Spirit men go astray, and though they study endlessly they cannot learn to know God and have not discovered what it is to rest in Him.

The man who has come to know the love of God himself loves the whole world and never murmurs at his fate, for temporary affliction endured for God's sake is a means to eternal joy.

The soul that is not humble and has not surrendered herself to the will of God cannot come to know anything, but flits from one idea to another and never prays with an undistracted mind or glorifies the majesty of God.

The soul that has surrendered humbly to God's will invisibly beholds God every second, yet finds no words for this, even to herself, and is unable to describe it, but only by experience comes to know the mercy of God, and to know when the Lord is with her. The soul has surrendered to Him like a little child who receives food each day but is ignorant whence comes that food. Thus it is with God the soul feels that all is well with her but cannot explain how this is.

Old age has come upon me, my body is grown feeble with the years and I would fain lie on my pallet, but my spirit rests not: my spirit reaches out with longing to her God, her heavenly Father. He has made us kin through His body and most pure blood and the Holy Spirit. He has given us to know what is eternal life. We know in part: the Holy Spirit is eternal life. The soul lives in the love of God, in the humility and meekness of the Holy Spirit; but we must give the Holy Spirit the freedom of our souls, that He may dwell therein, that the soul may be sensible of His presence.

He who on earth through the Holy Spirit dwells in the love of God will be with the Lord in the other world too, for love cannot melt away. But lest by reasoning we fall into error let us humble ourselves according to the word of the Lord:

'Become as little children, for of such is the Kingdom of Heaven.'

The Lord loves us more dearly than we can love ourselves; but the soul in her distress supposes that the Lord is forgetful of her, that He even has no wish to look upon her, and she suffers and pines.

But it is not so, brethren. The Lord loves us without end, and gives us the grace of the Holy Spirit, and comforts us. It is not the Lord's desire that the soul should be despondent and in doubt concerning her salvation. Believe and be sure that we continue in suffering only until we have humbled ourselves; but so soon as we humble ourselves there is an end to affliction, for the Spirit of God discloses to the soul, because of her humility, that she is saved.

Great glory be to the Lord that He loveth us so dearly, and this love is made known in the Holy Spirit.

O brethren, I beg and pray you in the name of God's compassion, believe in the Gospels and in the witness of the Holy Church, and you will, while still here on earth, savour the blessedness of paradise. For the Kingdom of God is within us; with the love of God the soul knows paradise.

My soul yearns after God and I seek Him in tears.

O merciful Lord, Thou seest my decline and my distress. I humbly entreat Thy mercy: pour upon my sinful self the grace of Thy Holy Spirit.

O Lord, grant me Thy spirit of humility that I lose not Thy grace again and weep not for it as Adam wept for paradise and for God.

4

Adam's Lament

ADAM, father of all mankind, in paradise knew the sweetness of the love of God; and so when for his sin he was driven forth from the garden of Eden, and was widowed of the love of God, he suffered greviously and lamented with a great moan. And the whole desert rang with his lamentations, for his soul was racked as he thought, 'I have distressed my beloved God'. He sorrowed less after paradise and the beauty thereof: for he sorrowed that he was bereft of the love of God, which insatiably, at every instant, draws the soul to Him.

In the same way the soul which has known God through the Holy Spirit but has afterwards lost grace experiences the torment that Adam suffered. There is an aching and a deep regret in the soul that has grieved the beloved Lord.

Adam pined on earth, and wept bitterly, and the earth was not pleasing to him.
He was heartsick for God, and this was his cry:
'My soul wearies for the Lord, and I seek Him in tears.
'How should I not seek Him?
'When I was with Him my soul was glad and at rest, and the enemy could not come nigh me;
'But now the spirit of evil has gained power over me, harassing and oppressing my soul,
'So that I weary for the Lord even unto death,
'And my spirit strains to God, and there is nought on earth can make me glad,
'Nor can my soul take comfort in any thing,

'But longs once more to see the Lord, that her hunger may be appeased.

'I cannot forget Him for a single moment, and my soul languishes for Him,

'And from the multitude of my afflictions I lift up my voice and cry:

' "Have mercy on me, O God. Have mercy on Thy fallen creature." '

Thus did Adam lament,

And the tears streamed down his face on to his breast, on to the ground beneath his feet,

And the whole desert heard the sound of his moaning;

The beasts and the birds were hushed in grief;

While Adam wept bitterly because peace and love were lost to all men on account of his sin.

Adam knew great grief when he was banished from paradise,

But when he saw Abel slain by his brother Cain Adam's grief was even heavier.

His soul was heavy, and he lamented and thought:

'Peoples and nations will descend from me and multiply,

'And suffering will be their lot, and they will all live in enmity and seek to slay one another.'

And his sorrow stretched wide as the sea,

And only the soul that has come to know the Lord and the magnitude of His love for us can understand.

I too have lost grace and call with Adam:

'Be merciful unto me, O Lord! Bestow on me the spirit of humility and love.'

O love of the Lord! He who has known Thee seeks Thee, tireless, day and night, crying with a loud voice:

'I pine for Thee, O Lord, and seek Thee in tears.

'How should I not seek Thee?

'Thou didst give me to know Thee by the Holy Spirit,
'And in her knowing of God my soul is drawn to seek Thee in
  tears.'

Adam wept:
'The desert cannot pleasure me; nor can the high mountains,
  nor meadow nor forest,
'Nor the singing of birds.
'I have no pleasure in any thing.
'My soul sorrows with a great sorrow:
'I have grieved God.
'And were the Lord to set me down in paradise again,
'There too would I sorrow and weep that I grieved my beloved
  God.'

The soul of Adam fell sick when he was exiled from paradise,
And many were the tears he shed in his distress.
Likewise every soul that has known the Lord yearns for Him
  and cries:
'Where art Thou, O Lord? Where art Thou, my Light?
'Why hast Thou hidden Thy face from me?
'Long is it since my soul beheld Thee, and she wearies after
  Thee and seeks Thee in tears.
'Where is my Lord?
'Why is it that my soul sees Him not?
'What hinders Him from dwelling in me?
'This hinders Him: Christ-like humility and love for my enemies
  are not in me.'

God is love insaturable, love impossible to describe.

Adam walked the earth, weeping from his heart's manifold ills,
  while the thoughts of his mind were on God;

And when his body grew faint, and he could no longer shed
   tears, still his spirit burned with longing for God,
For he could not forget paradise and the beauty thereof;
But even more was it the power of His love which caused the
   soul of Adam to reach out towards God.

I write of thee, O Adam;
But thou art witness, my feeble understanding cannot fathom
   thy longing after God,
Nor how thou didst carry the burden of repentance.
O Adam, thou dost see how I, thy child, suffer here on earth.
Small is the fire within me, and the flame of my love flickers
   low.
O Adam, sing unto us the song of the Lord,
That my soul may rejoice in the Lord
And be moved to praise and glorify Him as the Cherubim and
   Seraphim praise Him in the heavens
And all the hosts of heavenly angels sing to Him the thrice-holy
   hymn.
O Adam, our father, sing unto us the Lord's song,
That the whole earth may hear
And all thy sons may lift their minds to God and delight in the
   strains of the heavenly anthem,
And forget their sorrows on earth.

The Holy Spirit is love and sweetness for the soul, mind and
body. And those who have come to know God by the Holy
Spirit stretch upward day and night, insatiable, to the living God,
for the love of God is very sweet. But when the soul loses grace
her tears flow as she seeks the Holy Spirit anew.

But the man who has not known God through the Holy Spirit
cannot seek Him with tears, and his soul is ever harrowed by the
passions; his mind is on earthly things. Contemplation is not for

him, and he cannot come to know Jesus Christ. Jesus Christ is made known through the Holy Spirit.

Adam knew God in paradise, and after his fall sought Him in tears.

O Adam, our father, tell us, thy sons, of the Lord.
Thy soul didst know God on earth,
Knew paradise too, and the sweetness and gladness thereof,
And now thou livest in heaven and dost behold the glory of the Lord.
Tell of how our Lord is glorified for His sufferings.
Speak to us of the songs that are sung in heaven, how sweet they are,
For they are sung in the Holy Spirit.
Tell us of the glory of the Lord, of His great mercy and how He loveth His creature.
Tell us of the Most Holy Mother of God, how she is magnified in the heavens,
And the hymns that call her blessed.
Tell us how the Saints rejoice there, radiant with grace.
Tell us how they love the Lord and in what humility they stand before God.
O Adam, comfort and cheer our troubled souls.
Speak to us of the things thou dost behold in heaven . . .
Why art thou silent? . . .
Lo, the whole earth is in travail . . .
Art thou so filled with the love of God that thou canst not think of us?
Or thou beholdest the Mother of God in glory and canst not tear thyself from the sight,
And wouldst not bestow a word of tenderness on us who sorrow,
That we might forget the affliction there is on earth?
O Adam, our father, thou dost see the wretchedness of thy sons on earth. Why then art thou silent?

And Adam speaks:

'My children, leave me in peace.

'I cannot wrench myself from the love of God to speak with you.

'My soul is wounded with love of the Lord and rejoices in His beauty.

'How should I remember the earth?

'Those who live before the Face of the Most High cannot think on earthly things.'

O Adam, our father, thou hast forsaken us, thine orphans, though misery is our portion here on earth.

Tell us what we may do to be pleasing to God?

Look upon thy children scattered over the face of the earth, our minds scattered too.

Many have forgotten God.

They live in darkness and journey to the abysses of hell.

'Trouble me not. I see the Mother of God in glory—

'How can I tear myself away to speak with you?

'I see the holy Prophets and Apostles. and all they are in the likeness of our Lord Jesus Christ, Son of God.

'I walk in the gardens of paradise, and everywhere behold the glory of the Lord.

'For the Lord is in me and hath made me like unto Himself.'

O Adam, yet we are thy children!

Tell us in our tribulation how we may inherit paradise,

That we too, like thee, may behold the glory of the Lord.

Our souls long for the Lord, while thou dost live in heaven and rejoice in the glory of the Lord.

We beseech thee—comfort us.

'Why cry ye out to me, my children?

'The Lord loveth you and hath given you commandments.

'Be faithful to them, love one another, and ye shall find rest in God.

'Let not an hour pass without ye repent of your transgressions,
'That ye may be ready to meet the Lord.

'The Lord said: "I love them that love me, and glorify them that glorify me."'

O Adam, pray for us, thy children. Our souls are sad from many sorrows.

O Adam, our father, thou dwellest in heaven and dost behold the Lord seated in glory

On the right hand of God the Father.

Thou dost see the Cherubim and Seraphim and all the Saints

And thou dost hear celestial songs whose sweetness maketh thy soul forgetful of the earth.

But we here on earth are sad, and we weary greatly after God.

There is little fire within us with which to love the Lord ardently.

Inspire us, what must we do to gain paradise?

Adam makes answer:

'Leave me in peace, my children, for from sweetness of the love of God I cannot think about the earth.'

O Adam, our souls are weary, and we are heavy-laden with sorrow.

Speak a word of comfort to us.

Sing to us from the songs thou hearest in heaven,

That the whole earth may hear and men forget their afflictions . . .

O Adam, we are very sad.

'Leave me in peace. The time of my tribulation is past.

'From the beauty of paradise and the sweetness of the Holy Spirit I can no longer be mindful of the earth.

'But this I tell you:

'The Lord loveth you, and do you live in love and be obedient to those in authority over you.

'Humble your hearts, and the Spirit of God will live in you.

'He cometh softly into the soul and giveth her peace,

'And beareth wordless witness to salvation.

'Sing to God in love and lowliness of spirit, for the Lord rejoiceth therein.'

O Adam, our father, what are we to do?

We sing, but love and humility are not in us.

'Repent before the Lord, and entreat of Him.

'He loveth man and will give all things.

'I too repented deeply and sorrowed much that I had grieved God,

'And that peace and love were lost on earth because of my sin.

'My tears ran down my face. My breast was wet with my tears, and the earth under my feet;

'And the desert heard the sound of my moaning.

'You cannot apprehend my sorrow, nor how I lamented for God and for paradise.

'In paradise was I joyful and glad: the Spirit of God rejoiced me, and suffering was a stranger to me.

'But when I was driven forth from paradise cold and hunger began to torment me;

'The beasts and the birds that were gentle and had loved me turned into wild things

'And were afraid and ran from me.

'Evil thoughts goaded me.

'The sun and the wind scorched me.

'The rain fell on me.

'I was plagued by sickness and all the afflictions of the earth.

'But I endured all things, trusting steadfastly in God.

'Do ye, then, bear the travail of repentance.

'Greet tribulation. Wear down your bodies. Humble yourselves
'And love your enemies,

'That the Holy Spirit may take up His abode in you,

'And then shall ye know and attain the kingdom of heaven.

'But come not nigh me:

'Now from love of God have I forgotten the earth and all that
therein is.

'Forgotten even is the paradise I lost, for I behold the glory of
the Lord

'And the glory of the Saints whom the light of God's Countenance maketh radiant as the Lord Himself.'

O Adam, sing unto us a heavenly song,

That the whole earth may hearken and delight in the peace of
love towards God.

We would hear those songs:

Sweet are they for they are sung in the Holy Spirit.

Adam lost the earthly paradise and sought it weeping. But the Lord through His love on the Cross gave Adam another paradise, fairer than the old—a paradise in heaven where shines the Light of the Holy Trinity.

What shall we render unto the Lord for His love to us?

5

On the Mother of God and the Saints

MY soul trembles and is afraid when I consider the glory of the Mother of God.

She put not in writing the tale of her soul's affliction, and we know little of her life on earth. Her heart, her every thought, her entire soul were wrapped in the Lord; but to her was given something further: she loved mankind and prayed ardently for people, for newly-converted Christians that the Lord might sustain them, and for the whole world that all might be saved. This prayer was her joy and comfort on earth.

We cannot fathom the depth of the love of the Mother of God, but this we know:

The greater the love, the greater the sufferings of the soul.

The fuller the love, the fuller the knowledge of God.

The more ardent the love, the more fervent the prayer.

The more perfect the love, the holier the life.

O holy Virgin Mary tell us, thy children, of thy love on earth for thy Son and thy God. Tell us how thy spirit rejoiced in God thy Saviour. Tell us how thou didst look upon His fair countenance and reflect that this was He whom all the heavenly hosts wait upon in awe and love.

Tell us what thy soul felt when thou didst bear the wondrous Babe in thine arms. Tell us how thou didst rear Him; how, sick at heart, thou and Joseph sought Him three long days in Jerusalem. Tell us of thine agony when the Lord was delivered up to be crucified and lay dying on the Cross. Tell us what joy was thine at the Resurrection. Tell us how thy soul yearned after the Ascension of the Lord.

We long to know of thy life on earth with the Lord but thou wast not minded to commit all these things to writing, and didst veil thy secret heart in silence.

When the soul dwells in the love of God—how good and gracious and gay all things are! But even with God's love sorrows continue, and the greater the love the greater the sorrow. Never by a single thought did the Mother of God sin, nor did she ever lose grace, yet vast were her sorrows. When she stood by the Cross her grief was as boundless as the ocean, and her soul knew pain incomparably deeper than Adam's suffering when he was driven from paradise, for the reason that the measure of her love was beyond compare greater than the love with which Adam loved when he was in paradise. That she did not die was only because the strength of the Lord sustained her, for it was His desire that she should behold His Resurrection and live on after His Ascension to be the comfort and joy of the Apostles and the new Christian peoples.

We cannot discern to the full the love of the Mother of God, and so we cannot comprehend all her grief. Her love was complete. She had an illimitable love for God and her Son but she loved the people too with a great love. What then must she have felt when those same people whom she loved so dearly, and whose salvation she desired with all her being, crucified her beloved Son!

We cannot understand such things, since there is little love in us for God and man.

Just as the love of God is boundless and passes our understanding, so is her grief boundless and beyond our understanding.

Small and of no account is my mind, and poor and sickly my heart, but my soul rejoices and would fain set down if but a little concerning the Mother of God. My soul fears to speak but love constrains me to tell my gratitude for her compassion.

O if only we knew how the most holy Mother loves all men who keep the commandments of Christ, and how she pities and sorrows over sinners who do not repent! I had experience of this. Of a truth I say, speaking before God whom my soul knoweth: in the spirit I know the Most Pure Virgin. I never beheld her, but the Holy Spirit allowed me to know her and her love for us. Had it not been for her compassion I should have perished long ago; but she was minded to come to me and show me, that I might not sin. This is what she said: 'I find your ways ugly to look upon.' And her words, soft, quiet and gentle, wrought upon my soul. More than forty years have passed since then but my soul can never forget those sweet words, and I know not what return to make for such love towards my sinful self, nor how to give thanks to the good and forbearing Mother of the Lord.

Truly is she our advocate before God, and the very sound of her name gladdens the soul. But all heaven and earth too rejoice in her love.

Here is a wonderful thing which passes the understanding: she dwells in heaven and continually beholds the glory of God, yet she does not forget us, poor wretches that we are, and spreads her compassion over the whole earth and all peoples.

And this most pure Mother of His the Lord has bestowed on us. She is our joy and our expectation. She is our mother in the spirit, and kin to us by nature as a human being, and every Christian soul leaps to her in love.

Many are the marvels and mercies that I have witnessed at the hands of the Lord and His Mother, but there is nothing I can render in return for their love.

What could I give our most holy sovereign Lady for coming to me and bringing enlightenment, instead of turning from me in loathing in my sin? I did not see her with my eyes but the Holy Spirit gave me to know her by her words, which were filled with grace, and my spirit rejoices and my soul leaps to her in love, so that the mere invocation of her name is sweet to the heart.

One day when I was a young novice I was praying before the ikon of the Mother of God, and the Jesus Prayer entered into my heart and began to repeat itself there of its own accord. And another time I was listening in church to the reading from the prophet Isaiah, and at the words, 'Wash you, make you clean', I thought: 'Maybe at some time the Mother of God sinned, if only in thought.' And, marvellous to relate, in unison with my prayer a voice sounded clear in my heart, saying: 'The Mother of God never sinned, even in thought.' Thus did the Holy Spirit bear witness in my heart to her purity.

Call with faith upon the Mother of God and the Saints, and pray to them. They hear our prayers and even know our inmost thoughts.

Marvel not at this. Heaven and all the Saints live by the Holy Spirit, and in all the world there is nought hidden from the Holy Spirit. Once upon a time I did not understand how it was the holy inhabitants of heaven could see our lives, but when the Mother of God brought my sins home to me I realised that they see us in the Holy Spirit and know our entire lives.

The Saints hear our prayers and are possessed from God of the strength to help us. The whole Christian race knows this.

Father Roman, who was Father Dosiphey's son, told me that once when he was a boy he had to cross the river Don in winter, and his horse fell through an ice-hole and was just about to sink under the ice, carrying the sledge with it. He was a little lad at the time, and he cried at the top of his voice: 'St Nikolas, help me to pull the horse out!' And he tugged at the bridle and pulled the horse and the sledge out from under the ice.

And when Father Matthew, who came from the same village as I do, was a little boy he used to graze his father's sheep, like the prophet David. He was no taller than a sheep himself. His elder brother was working on the other side of a large field, and suddenly he saw a pack of wolves rushing at Misha—which was Father Matthew's name in the world—and little Misha cried out: 'St Nikolas, help!' And no sooner had the words left his lips than the wolves turned back and did no harm either to him or his flock. And for many a year after that the people of the village would shake their heads and say: 'Our Misha was terribly frightened by a pack of wolves, but St Nikolas saved him all right!'

The Saints were people just like ourselves. Many of them started with grievous sins but through repentance they attained the Kingdom of Heaven. And every one who comes to the Kingdom of Heaven does so through repentance which the Merciful Lord granted us by His sufferings.

In the Kingdom of Heaven the holy Saints look upon the glory of our Lord Jesus Christ; but through the Holy Spirit they see too the sufferings of men on earth. The Lord gave them such great grace that they embrace the whole world with their love. They see and know how we languish in affliction, how our hearts have withered within us, how despondency has fettered our souls, and they never cease to intercede for us with God.

The Saints rejoice when we repent, and grieve when men forsake God and become like unto brute beasts. They grieve to see people living on earth and not knowing that if they were to love one another the world would know freedom from sin; and where sin is absent there is joy and gladness of the Holy Spirit, in such wise that on all sides everything is pleasing, and the soul marvels that all is so well with her, and praises God.

The Saints in Heaven through the Holy Spirit behold the glory of God and the beauty of the Lord's Countenance. But in this same Holy Spirit they see our lives too, and our deeds. They know our sorrows and hear our burning prayers. When they were living on earth they learned of the love of God from the Holy Spirit; and he who knows love on earth takes it with him into eternal life in the Kingdom of Heaven, where love grows and becomes perfect. And if love makes one unable to forget a brother here, how much more must the Saints remember and pray for us!

The Lord bestowed the Holy Spirit on the Saints, and in the Holy Spirit they love us. The souls of the Saints know the Lord and His goodness towards man, wherefore their spirits burn with love for the peoples. While they were still on earth they could not without sorrow hear tell of sinful men, and in their prayers shed tears for them.

They were chosen of the Holy Spirit to pray for the whole world, Who gave them a well-spring of tears. The Holy Spirit gives His chosen such a wealth of love that their souls are possessed as it were by a flame of desire that all men should be saved and behold the glory of the Lord.

'I love them that love me, and them that honour me will I honour,' says the Lord.

God is glorified in the Saints, while the Saints have been given glory by God.

The glory which the Lord gives the Saints is so exceeding great that were men to see a Saint as he really is they would fall on their faces in veneration and awe, for man in the flesh is unable to bear the manifestation of heavenly glory.

Be not astonished at this. The Lord so loved His creature that He gave man abundantly of the Holy Spirit, and in the Holy Spirit man became like unto God.

But wherefore does the Lord so love man? Because He is Love itself; and this love is made known through the Holy Spirit.

By the Holy Spirit does man come to know the Lord his Creator, and the Holy Spirit with His grace fills his entire being: his soul, his mind and his body.

The Lord gave the Saints His grace, and they loved Him and clung to Him utterly, for the sweetness of the love of God prevents man from loving the world and its beauty.

And if it be thus here on earth how much more are the Saints in heaven united to the Lord in love! And this love is ineffably sweet and proceeds from the Holy Spirit, and all the heavenly hosts are nourished thereon.

God is love; and the Holy Spirit in the Saints is love.

By the Holy Spirit is the Lord made known. By the Holy Spirit is the Lord magnified in heaven. By the Holy Spirit do the Saints glorify God, and with the gifts of the Holy Spirit does the Lord give glory to the Saints, and this glory shall have no end.

To many people the Saints seem far from us. But the Saints are far only from those who have taken themselves away from them, and are very close to those who keep Christ's commandments and possess the grace of the Holy Spirit.

In heaven all things live and move by the Holy Spirit. But this same Holy Spirit is on earth too. The Holy Spirit lives in our Church; in the Sacraments; in the Holy Scriptures; in the hearts of the faithful. The Holy Spirit unites all men, and so the Saints are close to us; and when we pray to them they hear our prayers in the Holy Spirit, and our souls feel that they are praying for us.

How happy and blessed are we Orthodox Christians, that the Lord has given us life in the Holy Spirit; and He makes glad our souls. But we must guard Him soberly—a single evil thought and He forsakes the soul, and the love of God is then no longer with us; we have no more assurance in prayer and no firm hope that we shall receive that for which we ask.

In the Kingdom of Heaven where dwell the Lord and His most pure Mother abide all the Saints. There live our holy forefathers and the patriarchs who valiantly bore their faith before them. There dwell the Prophets who received the Holy Spirit and by their exhortations called the people to God. There dwell the Apostles who died that the Gospel might be preached. There dwell the Martyrs who gladly gave their lives for love of Christ.

There dwell the holy prelates who followed the Lord's example and took upon themselves the burden of their spiritual flock. There dwell the holy Fathers who lived lives of prayer and fasting, and those who assumed folly for Christ's sake, all of whom fought the good fight and so conquered the world. There dwell all the righteous who kept God's commandments and vanquished their passions.

Thither aspires my soul, to that wondrous holy assembly which the Holy Spirit has gathered together. But woe is me: inasmuch as I lack humility the Lord does not give me the strength to fight, and my feeble spirit flickers out like a tiny candle; whereas the spirit of the Saints burned with a bright flame, which the wind of temptation failed to extinguish but set burning more strongly still. They walked the earth and worked with their hands but their spirits continued with God, of Whom they were ever mindful. For love of Christ they endured every affliction on earth and feared no suffering, and thus they glorified the Lord. Wherefore the Lord loved them and glorified them, and granted them the eternal kingdom with Him.

The souls of the Saints, O Lord, hast Thou drawn unto Thyself, and they flow to Thee like gentle rivers.

The minds of the Saints attached themselves to Thee, O Lord, and are drawn to Thee, our Light and our Joy.

The hearts of Thy Saints were confirmed in Thy love, O Lord, and even in sleep they could not forget Thee, for sweet is the grace of the Holy Spirit.

6

We are God's children – we are in the likeness of the Lord

GOD created man from dust but He loves us as a father loves his children, and waits with longing for us to come to Him. The Lord so loved us that for our sakes He was made flesh, and shed His Blood for us and gave us to drink thereof, and gave us His most holy Body. Thus we have become His children, of His Flesh and Blood. We are in the likeness of the Lord in the flesh, as children to the end are like their father, and the Spirit of God is a witness to our spirit that we shall be with God to all eternity.

The Lord never ceases to call us to Himself: 'Come unto me, and I will give you rest.' He nourishes us with His most holy Body and Blood. In His mercy He schools us by His word and the Holy Spirit. He has revealed His mysteries to us. He lives in us and in the Sacraments of the Church, and leads us where we shall behold His glory. But this glory shall each man behold according to the measure of his love. The more a man loves the more ardently does he set his face towards God in yearning to be with the Beloved Lord, and therefore he will approach the nearer to Him; while the man who loves but little will have but little desire for the Lord; and the man who does not love at all will neither wish nor aspire to see the Lord, and will spend his life in darkness.

I weep for people who do not know God, who do not know His mercy. For to us the Lord showed Himself through the Holy Spirit, and we live in the light of His holy commandments.

Behold, a wondrous thing: grace gave me to know that all men who love God and keep His commandments are fulfilled with light and are in the likeness of the Lord; while those who go against God are full of darkness and are in the likeness of the enemy.

And this is natural. The Lord is Light, and He enlightens His servants, but they who serve the enemy have accepted the darkness of the enemy.

I once knew a boy who looked like an angel, so submissive and gentle was he. His little face was pink and white, and his clear blue eyes shone kind and tranquil. But when he grew up he began to lead a bad life, and lost the grace of God; and so by the time he reached the age of thirty he looked a mixture of man and fiend, wild beast and cut-throat, and the whole appearance of him was ruthless and dreadful.

I knew a girl too who was very beautiful—her face was so radiant and lovely that many were envious of her beauty. But through sin she lost grace, and then she was a painful sight.

Yet I have also seen other things. I have seen men arrive in the monastery with faces disfigured by sin and passion, but with repentance and a devout life they became good to look upon.

Another time the Lord let me see a priest—he was standing hearing confessions—in the image of Christ. Though his hair was white with age his face looked young and beautiful like the face of a boy, so inexpressibly radiant was he. In the same way I once saw a bishop during the Liturgy. I also saw Father John of Kronstadt, who by nature was an ordinary-looking man, until grace gave his face the beauty of an angel and made one want to gaze on him.

Thus sin disfigures a man, while grace brings beauty.

Man is made of the dust of the earth but God so loved him that He adorned him with His grace and fashioned him in the likeness of the Lord.

It is sad that because of our pride so few of us know this. Whereas if we were to humble ourselves the Lord would disclose this mystery to us, for He loves us dearly.

The Lord said to the Apostles: 'Children, have ye any meat?' What love those words reveal! But the Lord loves not only the Apostles but every one of us like that. When the Lord was told, 'Behold, thy mother and thy brethren stand without, desiring to speak with thee,' He answered and said: 'Whosoever doeth God's will, the same is my mother, and sister, and brother.'

There are people who declare there is no God. They say that because a proud spirit lives in their hearts, deceiving them with lies concerning the Truth and the Church of God. They are pleased with their cleverness, whereas in point of fact they do not even see that the thoughts they have are not theirs but proceed from the enemy. Whoever welcomes such thoughts into his heart, cherishing them, identifies himself with the evil spirit and will become like him. And God forbid that any man should die in that state!

Now in the hearts of the Saints lives the grace of the Holy Spirit making them kin with God, and they feel without a doubt that they are spiritual children of the heavenly Father, and therefore they say 'Our Father'.

The soul rejoices and is exceeding glad at these words. By the Holy Spirit she knows that the Lord is our Father. Created of earth though we be, the Holy Spirit dwells in us and makes us in the likeness of the Lord Jesus Christ, in the same way that children are like their fathers.

Man was formed of the dust of the ground—what good thing can there be in him?

Behold, God in His goodness adorned man with the grace of the Holy Spirit, and he became after the likeness of Jesus Christ, Son of God.

Great is this mystery, and great is the mercy of God towards man.

If all the people of the earth knew how deeply the Lord loves man their hearts would be filled with love of Christ and Christ's humility, and they would seek to be like Him in all things. But man cannot do this by himself, for it is only in the Holy Spirit that he can become like unto Christ. Man that is fallen purifies himself through repentance, and is made new by the grace of the Holy Spirit, and in all things becomes like unto the Lord.

So great is God's mercy towards us.

We thank Thee, O Lord, that Thou hast given us the Holy Spirit on earth, to teach the soul that which she never thought to know.

The Holy Spirit instructs us in the humility of Christ, that the soul may ever carry within her the grace of God which gladdens her and at the same time fills her with sadness for mankind; and she weeps and prays that all people may know the Lord and find delight in His love.

The man who has come to know the love of God through the Holy Spirit knows rest neither by day nor by night, and though his body succumb and he would fain lie on his pallet, even there the soul, unwearying, reaches up in longing towards God, her Father. The Lord has made us kin with Him. 'Thou, Father, art in me, and I in thee: may they also be one in us.' Thus the Lord by the Holy Spirit makes us one family with God the Father.

7

On the Will of God and on Freedom

IT is a great good to give oneself up to the will of God. Then the Lord alone is in the soul. No other thought can enter in, and the soul feels God's love, even though the body be suffering.

When the soul is entirely given over to the will of God the Lord Himself takes her in hand and the soul learns directly from God. Whereas, before, she turned to teachers and to the Scriptures for instruction. But it rarely happens that the soul's teacher is the Lord Himself through the grace of the Holy Spirit, and few there are that know of this, save only those who live according to God's will.

The proud man does not want to live according to God's will: he likes to be his own master and does not see that man has not wisdom enough to guide himself without God. And I when I lived in the world knew not the Lord and His Holy Spirit, nor how the Lord loves us—I relied on my own understanding; but when by the Holy Spirit I came to know our Lord Jesus Christ, Son of God, my soul submitted to God, and now I accept every affliction that befalls me, and say: 'The Lord looks down on me. What is there to fear?' But before, I could not live in this manner.

Life is much easier for the man who is given over to the will of God, since in illness, in poverty, in persecution he reflects thus: 'Such is God's pleasure, and I must endure on account of my sins.'

Thus for many years have I suffered violent headaches, which are hard to bear but salutary because the soul is humbled through sickness. My soul longs to pray and keep vigil, but sickness hinders me because of my body's demand for rest and quiet; and I besought the Lord to heal me, and the Lord hearkened not unto me. So, therefore, it would not have been salutary for me to have been cured.

Here is another case which happened to me, wherein the Lord made haste to hearken unto me and save me. We were given fish one feast-day in the refectory, and, while I was eating, a fish-bone found its way deep down my throat and stuck in my chest. I called to the holy martyr St Panteleimon, begging him to help me, as the doctor could not extract the bone. And when I spoke the word *heal* my soul received this answer: 'Leave the refectory, take a deep breath, fill out your cheeks with air, and then cough; and you will bring the bone up, together with some blood.' This I did. I went out, exhaled, coughed, and a big bone came up with some blood. And I understood that if the Lord does not cure me of my headaches it is because they are good for my soul.

The most precious thing in the world is to know God and understand His will, even if only in part.

The soul that has come to know God should in all things submit to His will, and live before Him in awe and love: in love, because the Lord is love; in awe, because we must go in fear of grieving God by some evil thought.

O Lord, by the power of the grace of the Holy Spirit vouchsafe that we may live according to Thy holy will.

When grace is with us we are strong in spirit; but when we lose grace we see our infirmity—we see that without God we cannot even think a good thing.

O God of Mercy, Thou knowest our infirmity. I beseech Thee, grant me a humble spirit, for in Thy mercy Thou dost enable the humble soul to live according to Thy will. Thou dost reveal Thy mysteries to her. Thou givest her to know Thee and the infinity of Thy love for us.

How are you to know if you are living according to the will of God?

Here is a sign: if you are distressed over anything it means that you have not fully surrendered to God's will, although it may seem to you that you live according to His will.

He who lives according to God's will has no cares. If he has need of something he offers himself and the thing he wants to God, and if he does not receive it he remains as tranquil as if he had got what he wanted.

The soul that is given over to the will of God fears nothing: neither thunder nor thieves *nor any other thing*. Whatever may come, 'Such is God's pleasure,' she says. If she falls sick she thinks, 'This means that I need sickness, or God would not have sent it.'

And in this wise is peace preserved in soul and body.

The man who takes thought for his own welfare is unable to give himself up to God's will, that his soul may have peace in God. But the humble soul is devoted to God's will, and lives before Him in awe and love: in awe, lest she grieve God in any way; in love, because the soul has come to know how the Lord loves us.

The best thing of all is to surrender to God's will and bear affliction having confidence in God. The Lord seeing our affliction will never give us too much to bear. If we seem to ourselves to be greatly afflicted it means that we have not surrendered to the will of God.

The soul that is in all things devoted to the will of God rests quiet in Him, for she knows of experience and from the Holy Scriptures that the Lord loves us much and watches over our souls, quickening all things by His grace in peace and love.

Nothing troubles the man who is given over to the will of God, be it illness, poverty or persecution. He knows that the Lord in His mercy is solicitous for us. The Holy Spirit, whom the soul knows, is witness thereof. But the proud and the self-willed do not want to surrender to God's will because they like their own way, and that is harmful for the soul.

Abba Pimen said: 'Our own will is like a wall of brass between us and God, preventing us from coming near to Him or contemplating His mercy.'

We must always pray the Lord for peace of soul that we may the more easily fulfil the Lord's commandments; for the Lord loves those who strive to do His will, and thus they attain profound peace in God.

He who does the Lord's will is content with all things, though he be poor or sick and suffering, because the grace of God gladdens his heart. But the man who is discontented with his lot and murmurs against his fate, or against those who cause him offence, should realise that his spirit is in a state of pride, which has taken from him his sense of gratitude towards God.

But if it be so with you, do not lose heart but try to trust firmly in the Lord and ask Him for a humble spirit; and when the lowly spirit of God comes to you you will then love Him and be at rest in spite of all tribulations.

The soul that has acquired humility is always mindful of God, and thinks to herself: 'God has created me. He suffered for me. He forgives me my sins and comforts me. He feeds me and cares for me. Why then should I take thought for myself, and what is there to fear, even if death threaten me?'

The Lord enlightens every soul that has surrendered to the will of God, for He said: 'Call upon me in the day of trouble: I will deliver thee, and thou shalt glorify me.'

A soul that is troubled about anything should inquire of the Lord and the Lord will give understanding: but this primarily in times of calamity and bewilderment. As a general rule we should be advised by our spiritual father, for this is a humbler way.

It is good to learn to live according to the will of God. The soul then dwells unceasingly in God, and is serene and tranquil;

and from the fulness of joy man prays that every soul may know the Lord, know His great love for us and how richly He gives us of the Holy Spirit, who rejoices the soul in God.

And all things are then dear to the soul, for all things are of God.

The Lord in His mercy gives man to understand that he must suffer affliction with a grateful heart. My whole life long I never once rebelled against affliction but accepted all things as physic from the hands of God, and I ever offered up thanks to God, wherefore the Lord enabled me to bear all affliction lightly.

No one on this earth can avoid affliction; and although the afflictions which the Lord sends are not great men imagine them beyond their strength and are crushed by them. This is because they will not humble their souls and commit themselves to the will of God. But the Lord Himself guides with His grace those who are given over to God's will, and they bear all things with fortitude for the sake of God Whom they have so loved and with Whom they are glorified for ever.

It is impossible to escape tribulation in this world but the man who is given over to the will of God bears tribulation easily, seeing it but putting his trust in the Lord, and so his tribulations pass.

When the Mother of God stood at the foot of the Cross the depth of her grief was inconceivable, for she loved her Son more than any one can realise. And we know that the greater the love the greater the suffering. By the laws of human nature the Mother of God could not possibly have borne her affliction; but she had submitted herself to the will of God, and the Holy Spirit sustained her and gave her the strength to bear this affliction.

And later, after the Ascension of the Lord, she became a great comfort to all God's people in their distress.

The Lord gave us the Holy Spirit, and the man in whom the Holy Spirit lives feels that he has paradise within him.

Perhaps you will say, 'Why is it I have not grace like that?' It is because you have not surrendered yourself to the will of God, but live in your own way.

Look at the man who likes to have his own way. His soul is never at peace and he is always discontented: this is not right and that is not as it should be. But the man who is entirely given over to the will of God can pray with a pure mind, his soul loves the Lord, and he finds everything pleasant and agreeable.

Thus did the Most Holy Virgin submit herself to God: 'Behold the handmaid of the Lord; be it unto me according to thy word.' And were we to say likewise--'Behold the servant of the Lord; be it unto me according to Thy word'--then the Lord's words written in the Gospels by the Holy Spirit would live in our souls, and the whole world would be filled with the love of God, and how beautiful would life be on earth! And although the words of God have been heard the length and breadth of the universe for so many centuries people do not understand and will not accept them. But the man who lives according to the will of God will be glorified in heaven and on earth.

The man who is given over to the will of God is occupied only with God. The grace of God helps him to continue in prayer. Though he may be working or talking, his soul is absorbed in God because he has given himself over to God's will, wherefore the Lord has him in His care.

There is a legend that a robber met the Holy Family when they were journeying into Egypt, but did them no harm; and when he saw the Child he said that were God to become flesh He would not be more beautiful than this Child. And he left them to go in peace.

What an astonishing thing that a robber, who like a savage beast spares no one, should neither annoy nor hurt the Holy Family! At the sight of the Child and His lowly Mother the robber's heart softened and was touched by the grace of God.

Thus it was with the wild beasts who grew gentle when they saw martyrs and holy men, and did them no harm. And even devils fear the meek and humble soul who vanquishes them by obedience, soberness and prayer.

Another thing to marvel at: the robber had pity on the Infant Lord, but the high priests and elders delivered Him to Pilate to be crucified. And this was because they did not pray and seek enlightenment of the Lord as to what they should do, and how.

So it often happens that leaders and their people desire good but are ignorant where it is to be found. They do not know that it is in God, and comes from God.

We must always pray to the Lord to tell us what to do, and the Lord will not let us go astray.

Adam was not wise enough to ask the Lord about the fruit which Eve gave him, and so he lost paradise.

David did not ask the Lord whether it would be a good thing if he took Bath-sheba to wife, and so he fell into the sins of murder and adultery.

So with all the saints who sinned: they sinned because they had not called upon God to enlighten and help them. St Seraphim of Sarov said, 'When I spoke of myself I was often in error.'

But there are also sinless mistakes of imperfection: we can observe such even in the Mother of God. St Luke tells us that when she and Joseph were returning from Jerusalem she did not know where her Son was, supposing Him to be journeying with their kinsfolk and acquaintances, and it was only after they had searched three days that they found Him in the Temple at Jerusalem, conversing with the elders.

Thus the Lord alone is omniscient, and each one of us, *whoever he may be*, must pray to God for understanding, and consult his spiritual father, that we may avoid mistakes.

The Holy Spirit sets us all on different paths: one man lives a life of silent solitude in the desert; another prays for mankind;

still another is called to minister to Christ's flock; to a fourth it is given to comfort or preach to the suffering; while yet another serves his neighbour by his goods or by the fruits of his labour—and all these are gifts of the Holy Spirit given in varying degrees: to one man thirtyfold, to another sixty and to some an hundred.

If we loved one another in simplicity of heart the Lord through the Holy Spirit would show us many miracles and reveal great mysteries.

God is love insatiable. . . .

My mind is arrested in God, and I leave writing. . . .

How clear it is to me that the Lord steers us. Without Him we cannot even think a good thing. Therefore we must humbly surrender ourselves to the will of God, that the Lord may guide us.

We all suffer here on earth and seek freedom, but few there are who know the meaning of freedom and where it is to be found.

I too want freedom and seek it day and night. I learnt that freedom is with God and is given of God to humble hearts who have repented and sacrificed their wills before Him. To those who repent the Lord gives His peace and freedom to love Him. There is nothing better in the world than to love God and one's fellow-man. In this does the soul find rest and joy.

O all ye peoples of the earth, I fall on my knees to you, beseeching you with tears to come to Christ. I know His love for you. I know and therefore I cry to the whole world. If one does not know a thing, how could one speak of it?

'But how may I know God?' you will ask. And I say that we have seen the Lord by the Holy Spirit. If you humble yourself the Holy Spirit will show our Lord to you too; and you too will want to proclaim Him to all the world.

I am an old man awaiting death. I write the truth for love of God's people over whom my soul grieves. If I should help but a single soul to salvation I will give thanks to God; but my heart aches for the whole world, and I pray and shed tears for the whole world, that all may repent and know God, and live in love, and delight in freedom in God.

O all ye peoples of the earth, pray and weep for your sins, that the Lord may forgive them. Where there is forgiveness of sins there is freedom of conscience and love, even if but a little.

The Lord does not desire the death of a sinner, and on him who repents He bestows the grace of the Holy Spirit, which gives peace to the soul and freedom for the mind and heart to dwell in God. When the Holy Spirit forgives us our sins we receive freedom to pray to God with an undistracted mind, and we can freely think on God and live serene and joyous in Him. And this is true freedom. But without God there can be no freedom, for the enemy agitates the soul with evil thoughts.

I will speak truth before the whole world: I am an abomination in the sight of God, and had not God given me His grace of the Holy Spirit I should despair of salvation. And the Holy Spirit instructed me, and so I write of God without difficulty, in that He inspires me to write.

I weep and sob with pity for mankind. Many people think to themselves: 'I have plundered and killed, used violence, slandered and led a wanton life, and done many other things.' And shame keeps them from the path of repentance. But they forget that in God's sight all their sins are as drops of water in the sea.

O my brethren the world over, repent while there is still time. God mercifully awaits our repentance. And all heaven and all the Saints look for our repentance. As God is love, so the Holy Spirit in the Saints is love. Ask, and the Lord will forgive. And when you receive forgiveness of sins there will be joy and gladness in your souls, and the grace of the Holy Spirit will enter into your souls, and you will cry: 'This is true freedom. True freedom is in God and of God.'

The grace of God does not take away freedom, but merely helps man to fulfil God's commandments. Adam knew grace but he could still exercise his will. Thus too the angels abide in the Holy Spirit and yet are not deprived of free-will.

Many people are ignorant of the way of salvation: they walk in darkness and do not see the Light of Truth. But He was, is and shall be, and in His mercy calls all men to Himself. 'Come unto me, all ye that labour and are heavy laden. Know me, and I will give you rest and freedom.'

This is true freedom—to be in God. And I did not know this before. Until I was seven and twenty I simply believed that God was, but I did not know Him; but when my soul knew Him by the Holy Spirit I was consumed with longing for Him, and now day and night I seek Him with burning heart.

The Lord wants us to love one another: in this—in love towards God and our fellow-man—lies freedom. In this lie both freedom and equality. With society as it is graduated on this earth there can be no equality; but that is of no importance to the soul. Not every one can be an emperor or a prince; not every one can be a patriarch or an abbot, or a leader; but in every walk of life we can love God and be pleasing to Him, and only this is important. And the man who loves God most in this world will have the most glory in the Kingdom. He who loves most will the most strongly yearn and reach for God, and be closest to Him. Each will be glorified according to the measure of his love. And I have discovered that love varies in strength.

When a man fears God lest he grieve Him in some way—that is the first degree of love. He who keeps his mind pure of intrusive thoughts knows the second degree of love, which is greater than the first. The third and still greater kind of love is when a man is sensible of grace in his soul.

The fourth and perfect kind of love for God exists when a man possesses the grace of the Holy Spirit both in soul and body. The body is then hallowed, and after death the earthly remains become relics. This is what happened in the case of the holy Martyrs and Prophets and venerable Fathers. The man who loves in this wise is proof against carnal love. He may lie beside a woman without feeling the smallest desire for her. Love of God is stronger than love of woman—to which all the world is attracted save those who are filled with the grace of God, for the sweetness of the Holy Spirit regenerates the entire man and teaches him to love God to the utmost. In the fulness of her love for God the soul has no contact with the world: though a man live on earth among other men, in his love for God he forgets everything that is of this world. But our trouble is that through the pride of our mind we do not continue in this grace, and so grace forsakes us, and the soul seeks it, weeping and sobbing, and saying:

'My soul longs for the Lord.'

8

On Prayer

WE eat and drink every day, yet on the morrow our bodies need drink and food again. In like manner the recollection of God's bounties never wearies the soul but disposes her still more to think on God. Or again: the more wood you pile on a fire the more heat you get, and thus it is with God—the more you think on Him the more are you fired with love and fervour towards Him. He who loves the Lord is always mindful of Him, and remembrance of God begets prayer. If you are forgetful of the Lord you will not pray, and without prayer the soul will not dwell in the love of God, for the grace of the Holy Spirit comes through prayer. Prayer preserves a man from sin, for the prayerful mind is intent on God and in humbleness of spirit stands before the face of the Lord, Who knoweth the soul of him who prays.

But the novice naturally needs a guide, for until the advent of the grace of the Holy Spirit the soul is involved in fierce struggle with her foes and is unable to disentangle herself if the enemy offer her his delights. Only the man with experience of the grace of the Holy Spirit can understand this. He who has tasted of the Holy Spirit recognizes the taste of grace.

The man who sets out without guidance to engage in prayer (imagining in his arrogance that he can learn to pray from books), and will not go to a spiritual director is already half beguiled. But the Lord succours the man who is humble, and if there be no experienced guide, and he turns to the confessor he finds, the Lord will watch over him for his humility.

Whoever would pray without ceasing must have fortitude and be wise, and he should consult his confessor in all things. And if your father-confessor has not himself trodden the path of prayer nevertheless seek counsel of him, and because of your humility the Lord will have mercy on you and keep you from all untruth. But if you think to yourself, 'My confessor lacks experience and is occupied with vain things: I will be my own guide with the help of books,' then your foot is set on a perilous path and you are not far from being beguiled and going astray. I know many such who reasoned thus and so deceived themselves, and who did not thrive because they despised their confessors. They forget that the saving grace of the Holy Spirit is at work in the Sacrament of confession. In such wise does the enemy delude those who fight the good fight—the enemy would have no men of prayer—but the Holy Spirit gives good counsel to the soul when we hearken to the advice of our pastors.

Think in this wise: the Holy Spirit dwells in your confessor and he will tell you what is right. But if you say to yourself that your confessor lives a negligent life, and how can the Holy Spirit dwell in him, you will suffer mightily from such thoughts, and the Lord will bring you low and you are sure to fall into temptation.

Prayer comes with praying, as it is said in the Scriptures; but prayer which is only a habit, prayer without contrition for our sins, is not pleasing to the Lord.

My soul yearns after the Lord, and I seek Him ardently, and my soul suffers thought of no other matter.

My soul yearns after the living Lord, and my spirit strains towards Him, my heavenly Father, my kin. The Lord made us His kin by the Holy Spirit. The Lord is dear to the heart—He is our joy and gladness, and our firm hope.

O Gracious Lord, mercifully seek out Thy creation and show Thyself to all men in the Holy Spirit, as Thou showest Thyself to Thy servants.

Rejoice, O Lord, every afflicted soul by the coming of Thy Holy Spirit, and let all who pray to Thee know the Holy Spirit.

O all ye people, let us humble ourselves for the sake of the Lord and the Kingdom of Heaven. Let us humble ourselves and the Lord will give us to know the power of the Jesus Prayer. Let us humble ourselves and the Spirit of God Himself will instruct the soul.

O man, learn the humility of Christ and the Lord will give you to taste of the sweetness of prayer. And if you would pray cleanly, be humble and temperate, confess yourself thoroughly, and prayer will feel at home in you. Be obedient, submit with a good conscience to those in authority; be content with all things, and your mind will be cleansed of vain thoughts. Remember that the Lord sees you, and be fearful lest you anywise offend your brother, whom neither dispraise nor grieve, even by a look, and the Holy Spirit will love you and will Himself be your help in all things.

If you would retain prayer you must love those who offend against you and pray for them until your soul is reconciled with them, and then the Lord will give you prayer without ceasing, for He giveth prayer to those who pray for their enemies.

For prayer our teacher is the Lord Himself, but we must seek to humble our souls. He who prays aright has the peace of God in his soul. The man of prayer should feel tenderly towards every living thing. The man of prayer loves all men and has compassion for all, for the grace of the Holy Spirit has taught him love.

The Holy Spirit is like a dear mother. A mother loves her child and has pity on it; and the Holy Spirit has pity on us, forgives and heals us, enlightens and rejoices us. And the Holy Spirit becomes known in humble prayer.

The man who loves his enemies soon comes to know the Lord in the Holy Spirit. But the man who does not love his enemies is to be pitied, for he is a torment to himself and to others, and does not know the Lord.

The soul that loves the Lord is unable not to pray, for she is drawn to Him by the grace she has come to know in prayer.

We are given churches to pray in and in church the holy Offices are performed according to books. But we cannot take a church away with us, and books are not always to hand, but interior prayer is always and everywhere possible. Divine service is celebrated in church, and the Spirit of God dwells therein, but the soul is the finest of God's churches, and for the man who prays in his heart the whole world is a church. However, this is not for all men.

Many people speak the words of their prayer, and like to read prayers from books; and this is good and the Lord accepts their prayers and is merciful to them. But if a man prays to the Lord but thinks of other things, the Lord hearkens not to his prayer.

The prayer of the man who prays from habit is always the same, whereas the prayer of him who prays fervently sees many vicissitudes: now he is engaged in struggle with the enemy, now with himself and his passions, now with other people; and in all this he has need of fortitude.

Ask counsel of the experienced, if such you find, and humbly entreat the Lord, and He will give you understanding because of your humility.

If our prayer is pleasing to the Lord, the Spirit of God bears witness in our soul. The Spirit of God is pleasant and tranquil. But in the past I did not know whether or no the Lord had received my prayer, nor how it was possible to tell.

Sorrow and danger have taught many people to pray.

A soldier came to see me in the storehouse: he was on his way to Salonika. My soul took a liking to him, and I said to him:

'Pray to the Lord that there may be less affliction in the world.'

And he replied:

'I know how to pray. I learnt in the war, when I was fighting. I prayed hard to the Lord to let me live. Bullets showered down, shells burst, and few of us were left alive; but I was many a time in battle and the Lord preserved me.'

As he spoke he showed me how he prayed and by the attitude of his body it was plain how he had been utterly wrapped in God.

Many people like to read good books, and this is right, but it is best of all to pray; while he who reads newspapers or bad books condemns his soul to go hungry—hungry because the food of the soul and her true satisfaction are in God. He who would pray freely and untroubled must keep himself in ignorance of the news in newspapers, nor should he read mean books or be curious to know details of other people's lives. All these things fill the mind with thoughts that stain, and when one would sort them out they further entangle and weary. Now in God are life, joy, gladness, and the Lord loveth us ineffably, and this love is made known by the Holy Spirit.

If you are minded to pray in your heart and are not able, repeat the words of your prayer with your lips and keep your mind on the words you are saying, as St John Klimakos explains. In time the Lord will give you interior prayer without distraction, and you will pray with ease. Some there are who have injured their hearts in their efforts to force their minds to pray in their hearts, so much so that afterwards they were unable to say the words of their prayer with their lips either. But do not forget the rule of spiritual life: God bestows His gifts on the simple, lowly and obedient soul. The man who is obedient and temperate in all things—in food, in speech, in movement—receives the gift of prayer from the Lord Himself, and prayer continues without difficulty in his heart.

Uninterrupted prayer is born of love, but fault-finding, idle talk and self-indulgence are the death of prayer. The man who loves God is able to keep Him in mind day and night since *no form of activity interferes with loving God*. The Apostles loved the Lord, and the world did not prevent them, though they were not forgetful of the world and prayed for it, and preached. True, Arsenios the Great was told to 'avoid people', but in the desert too the Spirit of God teaches us to pray for people and for the whole world.

Every one in this world has his task to perform, be he king or patriarch, cook, blacksmith or teacher, but the Lord Whose love extends to every one of us will give greater reward to the man whose love for God is the greater. The Lord gave us His commandment to love God with all our hearts, with all our minds, with all our souls. But without prayer who can love God? The mind and heart of man, therefore, must always be free to pray.

When we love anyone we like to think about that person, talk about him and be with him. Now the soul loves the Lord, as her Father and Creator, and stands before Him in awe and love: in awe because He is the Lord; in love because the soul knows Him for her Father; He is all mercy, and His grace more to be desired than aught else.

And experience has shown me that the grace of God makes prayer easy. The Lord loves us and in His mercy gives us prayer in which to talk with Him, repent and give thanks.

I have not the power to describe how greatly the Lord loves us. This love is made known in the Holy Spirit, and the soul when she prays knows the Holy Spirit.

For those who ask for my prayers I entreat the Lord with tears: 'Lord, give them Thy Holy Spirit, that through the Holy Spirit they may know Thee.'

Some there are who say that prayer beguiles. This is not so. A man is beguiled by listening to his own self, and not by prayer. All the Saints lived in prayer, and called others to prayer. Prayer is the best of all activities for the soul. Prayer is the path to God. By prayer we obtain humility, patience and every good gift. The man who speaks against prayer has manifestly never experienced the goodness of the Lord, and how greatly He loves us. No evil ever comes from God. All the Saints prayed without ceasing: they filled every moment with prayer.

When the soul loses humility she loses grace and love for God at the same time, and ardent prayer is extinguished. But when the soul stills her passions and grows humble the Lord gives her His grace, and she then prays for her enemies as for herself, and sheds scalding tears in prayer for the whole world.

O brethren, let us forget the earth and all that is therein! The earth entices us from contemplation of the Holy Trinity, Which our minds cannot apprehend but Which the Saints in heaven behold in the Holy Spirit.

We, for our part, should continue in prayer without imaginings, and ask of the Lord a humble spirit, and the Lord will love us and give us here on earth all things wholesome for soul and body.

O merciful Lord, give Thy grace to all the peoples of the earth that they may come to know Thee, for without Thy Holy Spirit man cannot know Thee and conceive of Thy love.

Little children, know the Creator of heaven and earth.

O Lord, send down Thy mercy on the children of the earth whom Thou dost love, and give them to know Thee by the Holy Spirit. With tears I implore Thee: Hear my prayer for Thy children, and grant that all may know Thy glory through the Holy Spirit.

All who led pure and sober lives, who were humble and obedient, who repented their sins have ascended into heaven, and there they behold our Lord Jesus Christ in glory, and hear the songs of the Cherubim, and think no more of earthly things. But we here below are swept about like dust before the wind, while our minds cling to the things of this world.

O how infirm is my spirit! A little wind can blow it out like a candle; but the spirit of the Saints glowed with fire like the burning bush, fearless of the wind. Who will give me such fire that I know rest neither by day nor by night from the love of God? The love of God is a consuming love. For the love of God the Saints bore every affliction: it was love of God gave them the power to work miracles. They healed the sick and restored life to the dead; they walked upon the waters, were lifted into the air during prayer, and by their prayers brought rain down from heaven; but all my desire is to learn humility and the love of Christ that I may offend no man and pray for all as I pray for myself.

9

On Humility

THE first year after I had received the Holy Spirit I thought to myself: 'The Lord has forgiven me my sins: grace is witness thereof. What more do I need?' But that is not the way to think. Though our sins be forgiven we must remember them and grieve for them all our lives, so as to preserve a contrite heart. I did not do this and ceased to be contrite, and suffered greatly from evil spirits. And I was perplexed at what was happening to me, and said: 'My soul knows the Lord and His love. How is it that evil thoughts come to me?' But the Lord had pity on me, and taught me the way to humble myself: 'Keep thy mind in hell, and despair not.' Thus is the enemy vanquished; but when my mind emerges from the fire the suggestions of passion gather strength again.

Fight the enemy with the weapon of humility.

Whoever like me has lost grace, let him wrestle manfully with evil spirits. Know that you yourself are to blame: you fell into pride and vanity, and the Lord in His mercy shows you what it means to be in the Holy Spirit and what it means to be at war with evil spirits. Thus the soul learns by experience the harm that comes of pride, and shuns vainglory and the praises of men, and evil thoughts. Then will the soul begin to recover her health and learn to retain grace. How can we tell if the soul is well or ailing? The ailing soul is full of pride, while the soul that is well loves the humility taught her by the Holy Spirit.

Though the Lord take her to heaven each day and show her all the heavenly glory in which He dwells, and the love of the Seraphim and Cherubim and all the Saints—even then with the knowledge of experience the humble soul will say: 'Thou, O Lord, showest me Thy glory because Thou lovest Thy creature; but do Thou give me tears and the power to thank Thee. To Thee belongeth glory in heaven and on earth, but for me—I must weep for my sins.'

The Lord showed great pity on me and made me understand that I must weep my life long. *Such is the way of the Lord*. And so I write now in pity for those who, like me, are full of pride and therefore suffer. I write that they may learn humility and find rest in God.

To learn Christ-like humility is a great good. Only to the humble does the Lord reveal Himself in the Holy Spirit, but if we do not humble ourselves we shall not see God. Humility is the light in which we may behold the Light which is God, as the Psalmist sang: 'In Thy light we shall see light.'

The Lord taught me to stay my mind in hell and not despair, and thus my soul humbles herself, but this is not yet true humility, which there are no words to describe.

There is a wide difference between the simplest man who has come to know the Lord by the Holy Spirit and even a very great man ignorant of the grace of the Holy Spirit.

There is a big distinction between merely believing that God exists, in seeing Him in nature or in the Scriptures, and knowing the Lord by the Holy Spirit.

The spirit of the man who has come to know God by the Holy Spirit burns day and night with love of God, and his soul can form no earthly attachment.

The soul that has not experienced the sweetness of the Holy Spirit rejoices in worldly vanity and praise, or in riches or power; but the Lord is the only desire of the soul that has come to know the Lord by the Holy Spirit, and riches and worldly fame count for nothing with her.

Great pains are needed, and many tears must be shed, to preserve the humble spirit of Christ; but without it the light of life is extinguished and the soul dies. The body may soon be made lean by fasting, but it is not easy or possible in a short space of time to subdue the soul, so that she is constantly humble. For seventeen years St Mary of Egypt wrestled with the passions, as with wild beasts, and only after that did she find peace; but her body was soon brought low—in the desert there was not even food for her to eat.

Our hearts are cold and we have no understanding of Christ's humility or love. True, this humility and love are made known by the grace of the Holy Spirit, but we do not believe it is possible to draw this grace to ourselves. To do so, we must desire it with our very souls. But how can I desire something of which I have no idea? All of us have some small idea of grace, and the Holy Spirit moves every soul to seek God.

O how needful it is that we entreat the Lord to give the soul the humble Holy Spirit! The lowly soul enjoys great peace, while the proud soul is a torment to herself. The proud man does not know the love of God and is far from Him. He is proud of being rich or learned or famous, but, alas, he is unaware of his poverty and ruin, for he does not know God. But the man who struggles against pride the Lord will help to overcome this passion.

The Lord said: 'Learn of me; for I am meek and lowly in heart.' Wherefore my soul wearies day and night, and I beseech God and all the Saints in heaven, and all you who have come to know the humility of Christ—pray for me, pray that the lowly spirit of Christ for which my soul weeps in longing may descend on me. I could not do otherwise than long for this humility which my soul once knew through the Holy Spirit, until I lost this gift, and so my soul yearns after it in tears.

Pride prevents the soul from setting out upon the path of faith. To the unbeliever I would give this counsel: Let him say,

'Lord, if Thou dost exist enlighten me and I will serve Thee with all my heart and soul.' And for such humility of mind and readiness to serve God the Lord will of a certainty enlighten him. But do not say, 'If Thou dost exist punish me', because if punishment should come it may be that you would not find strength to thank God and offer repentance.

When the Lord enlightens you your soul will feel His presence, will feel that the Lord has forgiven you and loves you. And this you will come to know of experience, and the grace of the Holy Spirit will bear witness in your soul to your salvation, and you will want to cry aloud to the whole world: 'How greatly the Lord loves us!'

Before he knew the Lord Paul the Apostle persecuted Him, but when he came to know Him he travelled the length and breadth of the earth, preaching Christ.

Unless the Lord grant him knowledge in the Holy Spirit man cannot know how greatly He loves us, for there is no earthly science can teach the human mind of the love the Lord has for men.

But to be saved we must humble ourselves, for the proud man, even were he to be set down in paradise, would not find peace there but would be discontent and say, 'Why am I not in the first place?' But the humble soul is filled with love and does not seek to be in the foreground. The humble soul wishes good to all men and in all things is content.

The vainglorious either fear evil spirits or themselves resemble evil spirits. But we should not fear evil spirits—we should fear vainglory and pride, for through them grace is lost.

The man who converses with evil spirits defiles his mind, while the man who dwells in prayer is enlightened of the Lord.

The Lord loves us greatly, yet we fall because we lack humility. If we would preserve humility we must mortify the flesh and accept the Spirit of Christ. The Saints waged bitter war against evil spirits, and conquered them through humility, prayer and fasting.

He who has humbled himself has vanquished his foes.

What must we do to have peace in soul and body?

We must love every man like our own selves. When you find another mind contending against your mind humble yourself and the strife will have done.

What must we do to have peace in soul and body?

We must be prepared at all times for death. When the soul remembers death she becomes humble and yields herself up to the will of God, desiring to live in peace and love with all men.

With might and main and to the last breath of life we must strive to preserve our first fervour, which many have lost and not recovered. To retain this fervour we must always remember death: for if the soul is even partly prepared for death she is not afraid, humility and repentance come, and earthly things are forgotten. The mind continues undistracted, and prayer is diligent.

The man who is mindful of death is not beguiled by the world. He loves his fellows and even his enemies; he is obedient and sober. And so peace is preserved in his soul, and the grace of the Holy Spirit comes. And when through the Holy Spirit you come to know God your soul will delight in the Lord, and you will love Him and will ever remember the sweetness of the Holy Spirit, and this is verily heavenly food.

At first when a men begins to work for the Lord grace gives him the strength to be zealous after good, all is easy and effortless; and seeing this, in his inexperience he thinks to himself: 'I shall continue thus zealously all my life long,' and at the same time he exalts himself above those who live carelessly, and begins to pass judgment on them. And so he loses the grace that was helping him to keep God's commandments. And he does not understand what has happened—everything was going so well with him, but now it is all so difficult and he feels no desire to pray. But he should not be afraid: it is the Lord in His mercy nurturing the soul. The moment the soul exalts herself above her fellows she is attacked by some thought or impulse unpleasing to God. If she humbles herself grace does not depart, but if she does not some small temptation follows to humble her. Should she again not humble herself a ravaging struggle with the passions will start up within her. If she still does not humble herself she will fall into a measure of sin. Should she once again fail to humble herself a great temptation will ensue, and there will be grave sin. And so it will go on until the soul humbles herself, when temptation will leave her; and if she brings herself very low a gentle peace will come, and all that is evil will disappear.

Thus the whole spiritual warfare wages round humility. The enemy fell from pride, and would draw us to perdition by the same means. The enemy praises us, and should the soul listen to his praise grace withdraws until she repents. Thus throughout her life the soul is occupied with the lesson of Christ-like humility. So long as she has not humility wrong thoughts and impulses will always torment her. But the humble soul finds the rest and the peace of which the Lord tells.

Fasting and abstinence, vigil and withdrawal into silence, and other exploits of spiritual discipline all help, but humility is the principal power.

Humility is not learned in a trice. That is why the Lord said: 'Learn lowliness in heart and meekness of me.' To learn takes time. And there are some who have grown old in the practice of spiritual endeavour, yet still have not learned humility, and they cannot understand why things are not well with them, why they do not feel peace and their souls are cast down.

When the peace of Christ enters the soul, then is she glad to sit like Job among the ashes and behold others in glory. Then does the soul rejoice to be worse than any. This mystery of the humility of Christ is a great mystery, impossible to unfold. From love the soul wishes every human being more good than she wishes herself, and delights when she sees others happier, and grieves when she sees them suffering.

The Lord loves man but He sends affliction that we may perceive our weakness and humble ourselves, and for this humility receive the Holy Spirit. With the Holy Spirit all things are good, all things are joyful, all things are well.

One man may suffer much from poverty and sickness but he does not humble himself and so his suffering profits him nothing. Whereas another who humbles himself will be content with every kind of fate, since the Lord is his riches and his joy, and all men will wonder at the beauty of his soul.

'My troubles are manifold,' you may say. But I will tell you —or, what is better, the Lord Himself says—'Humble thyself, and thou wilt see, even to thine own astonishment, that thine adversities will be transformed into peace, and thou wilt exclaim: "Wherefore did I so torment and fret myself?" ' But now you rejoice, for you have humbled yourself and the grace of God has come to you. Now were you to sit alone in poverty your joy would not forsake you inasmuch as in your soul is that peace of which the Lord said: 'My peace I give unto you.' Thus to every humble soul the Lord gives peace.

The soul of the humble man is like the sea: throw a stone into the sea—for a moment it will ruffle the surface a little, and then sink to the bottom.

Thus do afflictions disappear down in the heart of the humble man because the strength of the Lord is with him.

Where is thy habitation, O humble soul?

Who dwells in thee, and to what shall I liken thee?

Thou burnest bright like the sun, and thou art not consumed but with thy warmth thou givest warmth unto all.

The earth is thine, for the meek shall inherit the earth, said the Lord.

Thou art a flowering garden, and in the heart of the garden lies a fair dwelling wherein it pleases the Lord to take up His abode.

Thou art beloved of heaven and earth.

The Apostles, Prophets, Bishops and holy Fathers love thee.

The Angels, the Seraphim and Cherubim love thee.

The most holy Mother of the Lord loves thee, O humble soul.

The Lord loves thee and rejoices in thee.

The Lord does not manifest Himself to the proud soul. All the books in the world will not help the proud soul to know the Lord. Her pride will not make way for the grace of the Holy Spirit, and God is known only through the Holy Spirit.

Enlightened by Baptism, people believe in God; but there are some who even know Him. To believe in God is good, but it is more blessed to know God. Nevertheless those who believe are blessed too, as the Lord said to Thomas, one of the Twelve: 'Because thou hast seen me, thou hast believed: blessed are they that have not seen, and yet have believed.'

If we were humble the Lord in His love would show us all things, would reveal to us all mysteries, but our trouble is that we are not humble: we puff ourselves up and boast over trifles, and so make both ourselves and others unhappy.

The Lord, though He is merficul, oppresses the soul with hunger on account of her pride, and withholds grace from her until she has learnt humility. I was perishing of my sins, and would long ago have been in hell had not the Lord and His holy and blessed Mother taken pity on me. O her quiet, gentle voice! A voice from heaven, the like of which we shall never hear on earth! And so now I write in tears of the Lord of mercy, as He were my Father. It is sweet for the soul to be with the Lord.

Adam tasted the sweetness of this bliss in paradise when he saw the Lord with clear eyes, and we feel in our souls that He is with us according to His promise: 'Lo, I am with you alway, even unto the end of the world.'

The Lord is with us. What more could we desire? The Lord created man that we might live and bask in Him for ever; that we might be with Him and in Him. And the Lord desires to be with us Himself, and in us. The Lord is our joy and our gladness, and when pride causes us to withdraw from Him it means that we deliver ourselves up of our own accord to suffering. Anguish of heart, dejection and evil thoughts lacerate us.

O Lord, the cares of this world overshadow our minds, and we are not able to comprehend the fulness of Thy love. Do Thou enlighten us. To Thy compassion all things are possible. Thou hast proclaimed in Thy holy Gospel that the dead shall hear the voice of the Son of God, and shall live. Make our dead soul to hear Thy voice this day, and come to life in joy.

Tell the world, O Lord: 'The sins of all men are forgiven,' and they will be forgiven.

Hallow us, O Lord, and all men will be made holy by Thy Spirit and all Thy peoples will glorify Thee on earth. And Thy will will be done on earth as it is in heaven, for to Thee all things are possible.

The proud man fears reproach, while the humble man cares nothing. He who has acquired the humility of Christ would ever upbraid himself: it rejoices him to be abused, and grieves him to be acclaimed. But this humility of his is only a beginning: when the soul comes to know the Lord in the Holy Spirit, how humble and meek He is, she sees herself as the worst of all sinners and is happy to sit in shabby raiment among the ashes, like Job, beholding other men in the Holy Spirit shining in the likeness of Christ.

My heart is heavy for poor folk who do not know God. They take pride in being able to fly; but there is nothing wonderful in that—birds fly and glorify God. Yet man, God's creation, forsakes his Creator. But consider, how will you stand on the Day of Judgment? Whither will you flee, and where will you hide yourself from the face of God?

I pray God constantly for you, that you may all be saved and rejoice eternally with the Angels and Saints. Of you I beg this: repent and humble yourselves, make glad the Lord Who awaits you with longing and mercy.

Blessed is the humble soul: she is beloved of the Lord.

All heaven and earth exalt the humble Saints, and the Lord grants them the glory to be with Him. 'Where I am, there shall also my servant be.'

The humility of the Mother of God is greater than any, wherefore all generations on earth exalt her, and all the heavenly hosts serve her; and this His Mother hath the Lord given us to intercede for us and be our help.

There is no better thing than to live in humility and love. The soul then knows a great peace within her, and will not set herself above her neighbour. If we love our enemies there will be no room in our souls for pride, for in the love of Christ none is above the other. Pride like a burning fire consumes all that is good; but the humility of Christ passes description and is sweet. Did men but know this the whole world would be apprenticed to this science. Day and night, all my life long, have I striven after humility, yet am I not able to capture it. My soul ever reflects: I have not yet attained that which I desire, and I cannot rest, but I humbly entreat you, brethren, you who know the love of Christ—pray for me that I may be delivered from the spirit of pride, that the humility of Christ may take up her abode in me.

There are many kinds of humility. One man is obedient and has nothing but blame for himself; and this is humility. Another repents him of his sins and considers himself loathsome in the sight of God; and this is humility. But there is still another humility in the man who has known the Lord by the Holy Spirit.

When the soul by the Holy Spirit sees the Lord, that He is meek and lowly, she humbles herself utterly. And this is an especial humility, which there are no words to describe, which is made known only through the Holy Spirit. And were men to understand through the Holy Spirit what a Lord is ours all would be transformed: the rich would despise their riches, scholars their learning, and rulers their glory and power. Every man would humble himself and live in profound peace and love. And there would be great joy on earth.

When the soul has given herself up to the will of God the mind contains nothing but God, and the soul stands before God with a pure mind.

O Lord, teach us by Thy Holy Spirit to be obedient and sober. Give us Adam's spirit of repentance. Give us tears to weep for our sins. Give us to praise and thank Thee world without end. Thou didst give us Thy most holy Body and Blood that we might live with Thee for all eternity, and be where Thou art, and behold Thy glory.

O Lord grant all the people of the earth to know how greatly Thou lovest us, and to know the wondrous life Thou dost prepare for them that believe on Thee.

10

Concerning Peace and Grace

ALL men want peace; but they do not know how to attain it.

Paissy the Great, having lost his temper, begged the Lord to deliver him from irritability. The Lord appeared to him and said, 'Paissy, if thou dost not wish to get angry, desire nothing, neither criticize nor hate any man, and thou wilt have no anger.'

Thus every one who renounces his own will before God and other people will always be at peace in his soul; but the man who likes to have his own way will never know peace.

The soul that has surrendered herself to the will of God bears every affliction and every ill with ease, because in times of sickness she prays and contemplates God saying: 'O Lord, Thou seest my sickness; Thou knowest how weak and sinful I am. Help me to endure my sufferings and to thank Thee for Thy goodness.' And the Lord relieves her pain, and the soul feels God's help and is glad in the sight of God, and gives thanks.

If some misfortune befall you, reflect in this wise:

'The Lord sees my heart, and if this is His will all will be well, both for me and for others.'

And thus your soul will always be at peace. But if a man murmur against his fate he will never have peace in his soul, even though he fast and spend much time in prayer.

The Apostles were deeply attached to the will of God. In this manner is peace preserved. All the great Saints likewise bore with every affliction, submitting themselves to the will of God.

The Lord loves us, and therefore we need have no fear save of sin; for through sin we lose grace, and without God's grace the enemy will harass the soul as the wind harasses smoke or a dry leaf.

O Merciful Lord, grant us Thy peace as Thou didst give
peace to the holy Apostles: 'My peace I give unto you.'

How may we preserve peace of soul among the temptations of our times?

Judging from the Scriptures and the temper of folk today, we are living through the final period, yet must we still preserve our soul's peace, without which we cannot be saved—as St Seraphim said, who upheld Russia with his prayer. During his lifetime the Lord preserved Russia because of his prayer; and after St Seraphim another pillar reached up from earth to heaven, Father John of Kronstadt. Let us pause and consider Father John of Kronstadt, for he was of our day: we witnessed his prayers, whereas the others we did not know.

We remember how when his carriage was brought round after the Liturgy and he stepped into it to take his seat people surged about him seeking his blessing; and in all this hurly-burly his soul remained wrapped in God. His attention was not distracted in the midst of the crowd, and he did not lose his peace of soul. How was he able to achieve this?

He was not distracted because he loved the people and never ceased praying to the Lord for us:

'O Lord, grant Thy peace to Thy people.

'O Lord, bestow Thy Holy Spirit on Thy servants, that their hearts may be kindled by Thy love and their feet set upon the path of truth and goodness.

'O Lord, I would that Thy peace be among all Thy people whom Thou hast loved to the utmost, Thou who didst give Thine only-begotten Son that the world might be saved.

'O Lord, grant them Thy grace, that in peace and love they may come to know and to love Thee, and say like the Apostles on Mount Tabor, "Master, it is good for us to be with thee." '

Just as Father John of Kronstadt preserved his peace of soul by praying for mankind without cease, so do we lose our peace because we do not love mankind. The holy Apostles and all the Saints desired the salvation of the world and, dwelling among men, they prayed ardently for them. The Holy Spirit gave them strength to love mankind. As for us, if we love not our brother we cannot have peace.

Let every man think on this.

Glory be to the Lord that He did not leave us orphaned but has given us the Holy Spirit on earth. The Holy Spirit teaches the soul ineffable love for mankind, and compassion for all who have gone astray. The Lord had pity on those who went astray and sent His only-begotten Son to save them; and the Holy Spirit teaches this same compassion towards those who have erred who go to hell. But he who has not possessed himself of the Holy Spirit has no wish to pray for his enemies.

St Paissy the Great prayed for his disciple who had denied Christ, and while he was praying the Lord appeared to him and said: 'Paissy, for whom dost thou pray? Knowest thou not that he denied Me?' But the Saint continued to weep for his disciple, and the Lord then said to him:

'Paissy, thou hast become like unto Me in thy love.'

After this fashion is peace acquired, and there is *no other* way.

Though a man pray much, and fast, but has not love for his enemies he can have no peace of soul. And I should not even be able to speak of this, had not the Holy Spirit taught me love.

The soul that is sinful and a prey to the passions cannot know peace and rejoice in the Lord, even though she possess all the riches of the earth, even though she rule over the whole world. If a great king merrily feasting with his princes and sitting on the throne of his glory were suddenly to be told: 'O King, thou art about to die,' his soul would be troubled and would tremble with fear, and he would see his infirmity.

100

Yet how many poor men there are, who are rich only in their love for God and who on being told that they were about to die would reply in peace: 'The Lord's will be done. Glory be to the Lord that He has remembered me, and wants to take me to paradise where the first to enter was the thief.'

There are poor men who have no fear but meet death in peace, like Simeon the Just, who lifted up his voice in praise and sang: 'Lord, now lettest thou thy servant depart in peace, according to thy word.'

We must expound to our brethren gently and with love. Peace is lost if we vaunt or exalt ourselves above our brethren, if we find fault, if we enlighten otherwise than gently and with love; if we eat too much, or are indolent in our prayers. All these things cause us to lose peace.

But if we accustom ourselves to praying fervently for our enemies and loving them peace will always dwell in our souls, whereas if we feel hatred for our brethren, or find fault with them, our minds will be clouded and we shall lose our peace and the confidence to pray to God.

The soul cannot know peace if she does not explore God's law day and night, for this law was written by the Spirit of God, and from the Scriptures the Spirit of God passes into the soul, and the soul feels the delight and loveliness thereof and no longer has any desire to love earthly things; for love of earthly things ravages the soul until she grows despondent and unkempt, and has no wish to pray to God. Then the enemy, seeing that the soul is not in God, causes her to waver, and unrestricted he can instil what he will in the mind. The soul is then driven from one set of thoughts to another, so that she spends the whole day in this confusion and is unable to contemplate God with a single mind.

The man who carries the peace of the Holy Spirit in his heart spreads peace around him; but he who has a malevolent spirit spreads evil.

How can one in authority preserve peace if those under him are disobedient?

It is difficult and distressing for him but he should remember that, though they are unruly, still the Lord loves them and suffered and died for their salvation. He must pray fervently for them, and the Lord will give prayer to him who prays; and he of experience will know the assurance and love for God that comes to the mind. Although he be a sinful man the Lord will grant him to taste the fruits of prayer, and if he accustom himself to pray thus for those under him his soul will have deep peace and love.

If you are in authority, and have to sit in judgment on someone for doing wrong, pray to the Lord to give you a tender heart which the Lord loves, and your judgment will then be sound; but if you judge purely according to deeds there will be errors in your judgment, and you will not be pleasing to the Lord.

The purpose of judgment must be that the man you judge should mend his ways, and you must be compassionate with every soul, with every created thing, and in all ways have a clear conscience yourself. Then deep peace will reign in mind and soul. Let us live in peace and love, and then the Lord will hear us and give us whatever we may ask for that is profitable.

How can a subordinate preserve peace of soul if the man he works for is bad-tempered and malicious?

A man who is bad-tempered is himself suffering at the hands of an evil spirit. He is suffering because of his pride. If the subordinate realises this, and prays for the sick soul of his superior, the Lord, seeing his patience, will grant him forgiveness of his sins and prayer without ceasing. It is a great thing in the sight of God to pray for those who hurt our feelings and injure us. For this the Lord will grant us grace, and by the Holy Spirit we shall come to know the Lord, and then we shall bear every affliction with joy for His sake, and the Lord will give us love for the whole world. We shall ardently desire the good of all men, and pray for all as for our own souls.

The Lord commanded us to love our enemies, and the man who loves his enemies is like to the Lord; but we can only love our enemies by the grace of the Holy Spirit. Therefore so soon as any man affront you pray to God for him and you will preserve the peace in your soul and the grace of God. But if you murmur and inveigh against your superior you will become as angry as he, and the words of the prophet David will be fulfilled in you: 'With the pure thou wilt shew thyself pure; and with the froward thou wilt shew thyself froward.'

Peace in our souls is not possible if we do not beg the Lord with all our hearts to give us love for all men. The Lord knew that if we did not love our enemies we should have no peace of soul, and so He gave us His commandment: 'Love your enemies.' If we do not love our enemies we shall only now and then be easy, as it were, in our souls; but if we love our enemies peace will dwell in our souls day and night.

Guard the peace of the grace of the Holy Spirit in your soul. Do not lose it over petty trifles. If you give peace to your brother, the Lord will give you incomparably more; but if you injure him, affliction will inevitably fall upon your soul.

If a dissolute thought comes into your mind drive it off at once and you will preserve your peace of soul; but if you harbour it your soul will lose her love for God and you will no longer have confidence to pray.

If you renounce your own will you have conquered the enemy and your reward will be peace of soul; but if you cling to your own will you will be vanquished by the enemy and despondency will beset your soul.

The man who is covetous cannot love God and his neighbour —his mind and heart are intent on riches. The spirit of repentance is not in him, nor will he have a heart contrite for his sins, and his soul cannot know the sweetness of the peace of Christ.

103

The soul that has known the Lord would see Him within her at all times, for the Lord enters the soul in quietness and gives her peace, and is a silent witness to salvation.

If the kings and rulers of the nations knew the love of God they would never make war. War comes to us for our sins, not because of our love. The Lord created us in His love, and bade us live in love and glorify Him.

If those in high places kept the commandments of the Lord and we obeyed them in humility there would be a great peace and gladness on earth, whereas now the whole universe travails because of the ambition for power and the lawlessness of the proud.

I pray Thee, O Merciful Lord, let all mankind, from the beginning to the end of time, come to know Thee that Thou art good and merciful, that all nations may rejoice in Thy peace and behold the light of Thy countenance. Thy gaze is tranquil and meek, and draws the soul to Thee.

I brought nothing but sins with me to the monastery, and I do not know why, when I was still only a young novice, the Lord gave me the grace of the Holy Spirit in such abundance that both my soul and my body were filled with this grace like unto the grace of the Martyrs, and my body longed to suffer for Christ.

I did not ask the Lord for the Holy Spirit: I did not know about the Holy Spirit and how He enters the soul, nor what He does with the soul; but now it is a great joy for me to write of this.

O Holy Spirit, how dear art Thou to the soul! To describe Thee is impossible, but the soul is sensible of Thy coming, and Thou givest peace to the mind and delight to the heart.

The Lord said, 'Learn of me; for I am meek and lowly in heart: and ye shall find rest unto your souls.' The Lord is speaking here of the Holy Spirit, for in the Holy Spirit alone does the soul find perfect rest.

Blessed are we Orthodox Christians in that the Lord loves us dearly and accords us the grace of the Holy Spirit, and in the Holy Spirit gives us to see His glory. But to preserve grace we must love our enemies and offer thanks to God for all our afflictions.

There was a sinful soul that the Lord summoned to repentance, and this soul turned to the Lord and He in His mercy received her and showed Himself to her. The Lord is merciful beyond measure, and lowly and meek. Of His great goodness He remembered not her sins, and the soul was charged with love for Him and now strains towards Him as a bird in a cramped cage strains towards the green grove.

The soul of this man came to know God, God the merciful, the bountiful, the all-lovely, and was filled with love for Him, and in the great fire of her love reaches out always yearning towards Him, for the grace of the Lord is exceeding sweet and warms the mind and the heart and the whole feeble body.

And on a sudden the soul loses this grace of the Lord; and when this happens she reflects, 'I must have offended my Lord. I will entreat His mercy. It may be He will grant me that grace again, for my soul no longer desires aught in this world save the Lord.' The love of the Lord is such a burning love that the soul which has once tasted thereof has no other desire; and if she loses this love, or if grace decreases, what prayers the soul pours out before God in her hunger to possess His grace once more! When he realised that he had lost grace St Seraphim knelt on bare stone day and night for three years, beseeching God to be merciful to him, a sinner.

Every day we feed the body and breathe in air that it may live. But what the soul needs is the Lord and the grace of the Holy Spirit, without which the soul is dead. As the sun warms and gives life to the flowers of the field, and they reach up to it, so the soul that loves God is drawn towards Him and basks in Him, and in her great joy would have all men equally happy. For this did the Lord create us, that in heaven we might dwell eternally with Him in love.

Glory be to the Lord and to His compassion: He so loved us that He gave us the Holy Spirit Who teaches all good things and gives us strength to vanquish sin. The Lord in His great mercy gives us grace, and we must hold fast to this grace, that we lose it not, for without grace a man is spiritually blind. Blind is he who accumulates riches in this world; which means that his soul does not know the Holy Spirit, does not know how sweet He is, and so is captivated by the earth. But he who has known the sweetness of the Holy Spirit knows that it is beyond compare, and there is nothing on earth can captivate him, for he is held in thrall by the love of the Lord alone and finds rest in God and rejoices, and weeps with pity for mankind because all men have not come to know the Lord.

When the soul is in the Holy Spirit she is content and does not yearn after the things of heaven, for the Kingdom of God is within us: the Lord has come and taken up His abode in us. But when the soul loses grace she longs for what is of heaven and seeks the Lord with tears.

Till the advent of grace man lives his life and thinks that all is well and prosperous with his soul; but when grace visits him and dwells with him he sees himself quite otherwise, and losing grace again he realises his unhappy state.

The king's son went far afield to hunt and losing himself in the depths of the forest could not find his way back to the castle. Many were the tears he shed as he sought the path in vain. Caught in the wild woods, he was heartsick for his father the king and his mother the queen, for his brothers and sisters. How should he, a king's son, live in the wild depths of the forest? And the king's son wept bitterly for his old life in his father's palace and longed grievously for his mother.

Thus, and even more, does the soul yearn and mourn when she loses grace.

A country cock lives in a small yard and is content with his lot. But the eagle who flies beneath the clouds and beholds the blue horizons knows many lands, has seen forest and meadow, river and mountain, sea and city. If you were to clip his wings and put him to live with the cock in the farmyard—oh how he would pine for the blue sky and the crags of the desert!

Thus is it with the soul that has known grace and lost it: she is inconsolable in her grief and nowhere can she find rest.

The Lord did not leave us 'comfortless', as a dying mother must leave her orphaned children, but gave us the Comforter, the Holy Spirit, and He draws us to love God with an insatiable love and to yearn after Him and seek Him day and night with tears.

O how ill it goes with the soul when she loses her love and assurance! In sadness of heart she raises her cry to God: 'When shall I see the Lord again, and rejoice in His peace and love?'

What is thy lament, O my soul,
And why dost thou shed tears?
Is it that thou hast forgotten what the Lord has done
    for thee,
Who dost deserve every punishment?

No, I have not forgotten how great was the mercy the Lord
    poured on me,
And I remember the sweetness of the grace of the Holy
    Spirit,
And know the love of the Lord

And how sweet this love is for soul and body.

Why dost thou weep, O my soul,
If thou dost know the Lord and His ineffable love for
thee?
What more dost thou want of thy Master,
Who has manifested such great mercy to thee?

My soul desires never to lose the grace of the Lord,
For the sweetness thereof draws my soul without cease
To love her Creator.

When the soul falls away from grace she entreats the Lord
again for the mercy she once knew. The soul is harassed and torn
by evil thoughts, and she turns for protection to the Lord, her
Creator, and beseeches Him to grant her a humble spirit so that
grace shall not forsake the soul but shall give her strength to love
her heavenly Father without cease.

The Lord takes His grace from the soul and thus in His mercy
and wisdom does He school the soul for whose sake His arms
were stretched upon the Cross in agony, that she might be
humble. He allows the soul to show forth her intent in the
struggle with the enemy, but the soul of herself is powerless to
vanquish him; and so my soul is sorrowful and longs for the Lord
and seeks Him in tears.

Man of himself is not able to fulfil God's commandments,
wherefore is it said, 'Ask, and it shall be given you'. And if we
do not ask we torment ourselves and deprive ourselves of the
grace of the Holy Spirit; and without grace many things perplex
the soul because she does not comprehend the will of God.

To possess grace a man must be temperate in all things: in his
gestures, in speech, in what he lets his eyes look upon, in the
thoughts of his mind, in the food he takes. And every form of
temperance is furthered by the teaching contained in the word

of God. It is written, 'Man shall not live by bread alone, but by every word that proceedeth out of the mouth of God.'

St Mary of Egypt took a few grains of wheat from the hands of St Zosimos, saying, 'That is enough with the grace of God.' We should train ourselves to eat as little as possible, yet within reason, as our work permits. After meals we should feel like praying. That is the measure of moderation.

The soul that has lost grace yearns after the Lord and weeps as Adam wept when he was driven from paradise. And no one can bring her consolation, save God. Adam wept great tears and they ran down in torrents, wetting his countenance, his bosom and the earth beneath his feet; and he fetched deep, powerful sighs like the bellows in a smithy. 'Lord, Lord,' he lamented, 'take me into paradise again.'

Adam's soul was perfect in the love of God and he knew the sweetness of paradise, but his soul was unpractised and he did not resist when Eve tempted him, as the sorely-afflicted Job resisted when tempted by his wife.

What is thy desire, O my soul,
And why dost thou sorrow and shed tears?

I mourn for the Lord that I have not seen this long while,
And no one can comfort my grieving after Him.
He gave me to know His mercy,
And I would have Him abide in me for ever.

When the soul is full of the love of God, out of the infinity of her joy she sorrows and prays in tears for the whole world that all men may come to know their Lord and heavenly Father. There is no rest for her, nor does she desire rest, until all mankind delights in the grace of His love.

When grace is in us we are truly humble, wise, submissive, meek and pleasing to God and man; but when we lose grace we wither away like a shoot cut from the vine.

The man who does not love his brother, for whom the Lord died in great suffering, has fallen from the Vine (which is the Lord); but the man who wrestles against sin the Lord will help.

Guard the grace of God: with grace life is easy. With God all is well, all is pleasant and joyous: the soul is at peace in God and walks, as it were, in a fair garden in which live the Lord and the Mother of God. Without grace man is but sinful clay; but with the grace of God the mind of man is like unto the angels who serve and love God.

When grace is present it is easy to love God and pray day and night; but the wise soul will bear arid periods too, trusting firmly in the Lord, and knowing that He will not confound her hopes but will turn to her in His good time. The grace of God is sometimes swift to come, sometimes long withheld; but the wise soul humbles herself and loves her neighbour and meekly bears her cross, and thus overcomes the attempts of the enemy to sever her from God.

Blessed are they who are concerned day and night to please the Lord and become worthy of His love: they come by experience to feel and know the grace of the Holy Spirit.

Glory be to the Lord that He gives us to discern the advent of grace, and teaches us to know wherefore grace comes and wherefore is lost. He who keeps all the commandments will always feel grace present in his soul, if only in small measure. But grace is easily lost through vanity, through a single proud thought. We may fast and pray much, do much good, but if with this we are puffed up we shall be like drums that thunder but are empty within. Vanity deals destruction to the soul, and much experience and a long struggle is required to vanquish it. In the monastery I learned of experience and from the Scriptures of the harm wrought by vanity, and now day and night I beseech the Lord for the humility of Christ. This is a great matter continually to be learned.

Fierce is the war we wage; yet it is a wise war and a simple one. If the soul grows to love humility, then all the snares of our enemies are overturned and his fortresses taken. In this spiritual warfare of ours we must look to the state of our ammunition and provender. Our ammunition is our humility; our provender— the grace of God. If we lose these, the enemy will defeat us.

The war is a stubborn war, but only for the proud: the humble find it easy because they love the Lord and He gives them the powerful armament of the grace of the Holy Spirit, of which our enemies are afraid, for it scorches them with fire.

Here now is the shortest, the easiest way to salvation:

Be obedient and sober. do not find fault, and keep mind and heart from evil thoughts. Remember that all men are good and beloved of the Lord. For such humility the grace of the Holy Spirit will dwell in you, and cause you to exclaim, 'How merciful is the Lord!'

But if you find fault and are rebellious, if you want your own way, your soul will fail and you will cry: 'The Lord has forgotten me!' But it is not the Lord who has forgotten you: it is you who have forgotten that you must humble yourself, and so the grace of God abides not in your soul. Into the humble soul, now, this grace enters with ease, bringing peace and rest in God. The Mother of God was perfect humility, wherefore is she glorified in heaven and on earth; and every one who humbles himself will be glorified of God and will behold the glory of the Lord.

A marvellous thing: by the Holy Spirit man comes to know the Lord, his Creator; and blessed are they who serve Him, for He has said: 'Where I am, there shall also my servant be,' and he shall 'behold my glory'.

And if it be so here on earth, how much more do the Saints in heaven love the Lord in the Holy Spirit and glorify Him! And this love is an unutterable love.

The soul that has known the Holy Spirit will understand what I write of.

Why does the Lord love us so? We are all sinful men, and (in the words of St John) 'the whole world lieth in wickedness'. Why should He love us?

The Lord Himself is *all love*.

As the sun warms the earth, so the grace of the Holy Spirit warms the soul to love the Lord, and she yearns for Him and seeks Him in tears.

How should I not seek Thee? Inscrutable Thou didst reveal Thyself to my soul and enthralled her by Thy love, and the grace of the Holy Spirit delighted my soul, and she cannot forget.

How shall we forget the Lord, when He is within us? And the Apostles preached to the peoples: 'May Christ be formed in you.'

O that the whole world knew the Lord and His love for us, and how sweet is this love, and how all the heavenly host lives by it, and how all things are set in motion by the Holy Spirit, and how the Lord is magnified for His sufferings, and how all the Saints glorify Him!

And there shall be no end to this glory.

The Lord rejoices in the soul that repents humbly, and gives her the grace of the Holy Spirit. I know of a certain novice who received the Holy Spirit after six months in the monastery. Others waited ten years; while still others wait forty or more years before knowing grace. But *no one* could retain this grace, because we are not humble.

The soul that has come to know God through the Holy Spirit surges upwards to Him: the memory of God tugs at her and the world is forgotten. And when the soul remembers the world her ardent desire is for all men to know God with her, and she prays for the whole world. The Holy Spirit Himself moves her to pray that all men may repent and know God, how merciful He is.

Let us humble ourselves, brethren, and the Lord will love us. We know by the grace the Lord gives the soul that He loves us. When there is grace in the soul, even a small measure, the soul loves the Lord and her fellow-men, and has peace within herself. But there is a greater love, and then the soul forgets the whole world.

Blessed is he who does not lose the grace of God but goes from strength to strength. (I lost the grace I knew but the Lord took pity on me and in His unique mercy gave me more grace.)

How infirm is the soul! Without God's grace we are like cattle, but with grace man is great in the sight of God.

Men set much store by earthly knowledge and take pride in knowing the princes of this world, rejoicing if they can claim friendship, but the truly great thing is to know the Lord and His will.

With all your might, brethren, humble your souls, that the Lord may love you and have mercy on you. But His grace will not remain in us if we do not love our enemies.

By the Holy Spirit my soul came to know the Lord, and therefore it is pleasant and easy for me to think on Him and on the works of God; but without the Holy Spirit the soul has no life, even though she has informed herself of all the knowledge of the world.

If people only knew there existed a spiritual science they would fling aside all their technics and knowledge, to contemplate the Lord. The beauty of the Lord captivates the soul, who is drawn to Him, and her eternal and only desire is to dwell with Him. The soul then looks on all the kingdoms of the earth as insubstantial as clouds floating across the sky.

The Lord said: 'I am in the Father, and the Father is in me,' and 'ye are in me, and I in you.' Our souls feel the Lord in us, and so we cannot forget Him for a single moment.

What mercy is this—that the Lord desires us to be in Him and in the Father!

But what have we done for Thee, Lord, or in what have we pleased Thee, that Thou dost wish to be in us, and for us to be in Thee? We have crucified Thee on the Cross with our sins, and dost Thou still want us to be with Thee? O how great is Thy mercy! I see Thy mercy spread over me. I am deserving of hell and every torment, yet Thou dost give me the grace of the Holy Spirit.

And if Thou hast vouchsafed to my sinful self to know Thee by the Holy Spirit, then I beseech Thee, O Lord, let the whole people come to know Thee.

11

Spiritual Warfare

ALL those who would follow our Lord Jesus Christ are engaged in spiritual warfare. The Saints by long experience learned from the grace of the Holy Spirit how to wage this war. The Holy Spirit appointed their footsteps and gave them understanding and the strength to overcome the enemy; but without the Holy Spirit the soul is incapable even of starting out upon the race, for she neither knows nor understands who and where her enemies are.

Blessed are we, Orthodox Christians, because we live under the protection of God's mercy. It is not difficult for us to wage this war: the Lord had pity on us and gave us the Holy Spirit, Who abides in our Church. Our only sorrow is that not every one knows God and how greatly He loves us. The man who prays is conscious of this love, and the Spirit of God bears witness in his soul to salvation.

Our battle rages every day and every hour.

If you have upbraided or passed judgment on or vexed your brother, your peace is lost. If you have been boastful, or have exalted yourself above your fellows, you have lost grace. If you do not drive away forthwith the wanton thought that comes to you your soul will lose the love of God and confidence in prayer. If you are fond of power, or of money, you will never come to know the love of God. If you have followed your own will, then you are conquered by the enemy, and despondency will come upon your soul. If you hate your fellow it means that you have fallen away from God, and an evil spirit has taken possession of you.

But if you will do good unto your brother you will gain rest for your conscience. If you subdue your own will your enemies will be driven off and you will receive peace in your soul.

If you forgive your brother the affronts he puts upon you, and love your enemies, then you will receive forgiveness for your sins, and the Lord will let you come to know the love of the Holy Spirit.

And when you have humbled yourself entirely you will find perfect rest in God.

Let us love our fellows, and the Lord will love us. Think not, O my soul, that the Lord loveth Thee if thou dost look askance upon any man. Rather is it then that thou art beloved of the devils, in that thou hast become their servant; but be not slow to repent, and ask the Lord for strength to love thy brother, and thou wilt then see that there is peace in thy soul.

With all your might ask the Lord for humility and brotherly love, for to him who loves his brother the Lord giveth freely of His grace. Make trial with yourself: ask God one day for brotherly love, and the next day live without love, and you will see the difference. The spiritual fruits of love are plain: peace and joy in the soul, with all men dear to you, and you shed abundant tears for your fellow-man and for every thing that hath breath and all creation.

Often a single sympathetic greeting will work a happy change in the soul; and, contrariwise, one unfriendly look, and grace and the love of God are gone. When that happens make haste to repent, that the peace of God may return to your soul.

Alas that I did not live a good life in the days of my youth and follow in the steps of my patron saint, Simeon Stylites. A wonderful life was his. He was seven years old when the Lord appeared to him, and he forthwith recognized the Lord and asked Him: 'Lord, how did they crucify Thee?' The Lord stretched out His arms and said: 'Thus did they crucify Me;

but it was My desire. And do thou crucify thyself with Me every day.'

Thus must we urge ourselves all our lives to do good, and above all must we forgive others their trespasses, and the Lord will then not be mindful of our own sins, and will give us the grace of the Holy Spirit.

St John the Divine declares that God's commandments are not grievous but a light burden. But they are light only where there is love—where love is not present everything is difficult. Therefore preserve love and lose it not, for though it is possible to recover love this can only be at the cost of many tears and prayers, and without love life on earth is hard. To continue in malice is death to the soul, from which may the Lord save us.

Long was I in torment, ignorant of the ways of the Lord, but now, after many years and much tribulation, and through the Holy Spirit, I have come to know God's will. All things whatsoever the Lord commanded must be fulfilled with exactitude, for this is the path to the Kingdom of Heaven, where we shall behold God. But do not think about seeing God: rather humble yourself and let your thought be that when you die you will be cast into a dark prison, and there languish and pine for the Lord. When we weep and humble our souls the grace of God preserves us, whereas if we forsake weeping and humility we may be led astray by intrusive thoughts or visions. The humble soul neither has nor desires to have visions, but prays God with an undisturbed mind; while the mind that is puffed up is not free from intrusive thoughts and imaginings, and may even reach the point of beholding devils and discoursing with them. I write of this because I myself have been in a like unhappy state.

Twice was I beguiled. The first time was at the beginning, when I was a young novice, and came about because of my inexperience; and the Lord was swift to forgive me. But the second occasion was due to pride, and that time I suffered long torment before the Lord healed me for the sake of my spiritual father's prayers. It all befell after I had accepted a certain vision. I revealed this vision to four men wise in the spirit, and not one of them told me that what I had seen was of the enemy, though vainglory had me in its clutches. But afterwards I came to understand where I had gone wrong, for devils started appearing to me again, not only by night but by day too. My soul saw them but I was not afraid, because I felt the grace of God with me. And thus for many years I suffered from them; and had the Lord not given me to know Him through the Holy Spirit, and had it not been for the help of our kindly and most holy Lady, I should have despaired of my salvation; but now my soul trusts firmly in God's compassion, though according to my deeds I am deserving of torment both on earth and in hell.

For a long while I was unable to make out what had befallen me. I thought within myself: 'I do not find fault with others; I harbour no evil thoughts; I perform my task of obedience punctually; I am abstinent in food; I pray without ceasing— why then do devils frequent me? I see I am in error but cannot fathom where, I say my prayers, and the devils go away for a time, but afterwards they come back again.' And my soul continued long in this conflict. I talked about it to some of the *startzy*. They were silent. And I stayed at a loss.

And lo, one night I was sitting in my cell and suddenly it was filled with devils. I started to pray fervently, and the Lord drove them away, but they came back again. Then I got to my feet ready to bow down before the ikons, with devils all round me and one of them standing out in front so that I could not bow down before the ikons without appearing to be bowing to him. I sat down again and said:

'Lord, Thou seest that I desire to pray to Thee with a pure mind but the devils will not let me. Tell me what I must do that they may leave me.'

And the Lord's reply came in my soul:

'The proud always suffer from devils.'

'Lord,' I say, 'Thou art merciful. My soul knoweth Thee. Tell me what I must do that my soul may grow humble?'

And the Lord answered me in my soul:

'Keep thy mind in hell, and despair not.'

O compassion of God! I am an abomination before God and man, yet thus does the Lord love me and give me understanding and heal me, and Himself teaches my soul humility and love, patience and obedience, and has poured out the fulness of His mercy upon me.

Since then I have kept my mind in hell, and I burn in the sombre fire, yearning after the Lord and seeking Him in tears and saying:

'Soon shall I die and take my abode in the dark prison of hell. I shall burn alone in longing for the Lord, and lament: "Where is my Lord, whom my soul knoweth?" '

And I had great profit from these thoughts: my mind was made clean and my soul found rest.

O wonder! The Lord bade me keep my mind in hell and not despair. So close is He to us: 'Lo, I am with you . . . even unto the end of the world,' and 'I will deliver thee, and thou shalt glorify me.'

So soon as the Lord lays His hand upon the soul she becomes a new being; but this is intelligible only to those who have experience, for without the Holy Spirit it is impossible to come to knowledge of what is of heaven, and this Spirit on earth is given of the Lord.

Who shall describe the joy of knowing the Lord and of reaching out towards Him day and night, insatiably? O how blessed and happy are we Christians! There is nothing more precious than to know God; and nothing worse than not to know Him. But he too is blessed who, though he does not know, yet believes.

I beseech all men—let us make haste to repent, and we shall perceive the mercy of the Lord. And I beseech those who see visions and put their trust in them to understand that this is a source of evil pride and, side by side with pride, sweet vanity, in which there is no lowly spirit of repentance, and that is where the trouble lies, for without humility it is impossible to vanquish the enemy.

I myself was twice deluded. Once the enemy showed me light and the thought tempted me: 'Accept what thou dost see: it proceeds from grace.' Another time I accepted a vision and suffered greatly on that account. Once, at the end of vespers when the choir were started on 'Let every thing that hath breath praise the Lord', I heard King David in heaven singing the praises of God. I was standing in the choir and it seemed to me that there was neither roof nor dome, and that I was looking at the open sky. I spoke of this to four men of God but not one told me that the enemy had made mock of me, while I myself thought that devils could not be singing the praises of God, and that therefore my vision could not be from the enemy. But I was beguiled by vanity and began to see devils again. Then I knew that I had been deceived, and I made full disclosure to my confessor and asked him for his prayers; and because of his prayers I am now saved, and ever beseech the Lord to grant me a spirit of humility. And were I to be asked what would I have of God, what gifts, I should answer: 'The spirit of humility in which the Lord rejoices above all things.' Because of her humility the Virgin Mary became the Mother of God and is glorified in heaven and on earth above all others. She committed herself entirely to the will of God. 'Behold the handmaid of the Lord,' she said; and we all must try to do likewise.

If you feel an evil spirit working within you, even so do not quail but confess yourself throughly and earnestly, and entreat a lowly spirit of the Lord, and the Lord will give without fail.

Then, according to the measure of your humility you will be sensible of grace within you; and when your soul finally humbles herself, then will you attain perfect rest.

And this is the war man wages his life long.

The soul that has come to know the Lord through the Holy Spirit does not take fright if afterwards she suffer beguilement, but remembering the love of God, and knowing that conflict with the enemy is loosed on her because of vanity and pride, she humbles herself and begs the Lord for healing, and the Lord heals—sometimes swiftly, sometimes slowly and gradually. The obedient man who puts his trust in his confessor and not in himself will quickly be healed of any harm done to him by the enemy, whereas the man without obedience will not grow better.

Prayer to be clear and unsullied requires inner peace; but peace cannot exist in the soul without obedience and temperance.

The holy Fathers ranked obedience above fasting and prayer since a man who knows not obedience may think of himself as a spiritual wrestler and man of prayer, whereas he who has excised his self-will and put himself under obedience in all things to his *staretz* and his confessor is serene in mind.

The soul's war with the enemy lasts until death. And, whereas in ordinary warfare only the body suffers, in our war, which is harder and more dangerous, the soul may perish.

On account of my pride the Lord twice let the enemy create strife in me, in such wise that my soul stood in hell; and I can say that a soul will hold out if she be courageous, but if not she may perish for all eternity. To all who may find themselves in the misfortune which overtook me I write now: Have courage and stand fast. Hope firmly in God, and the enemy will not hold out, for the Lord hath overcome him. By the grace of God I have come to know that the Lord mercifully watches over us, and not one prayer nor a single good thought is lost with God. The Lord often seems not to hear us; but that is only because we are proud and what we ask would not be for our good. Pride is difficult to detect in oneself, but the Lord leaves the proud to be tormented by their impotence until they humble themselves. But when the soul humbles herself the enemy is vanquished, and the soul finds deep rest in God.

Who is there can realise what paradise is? He who bears within him the Holy Spirit can realise it in part, since paradise is the Kingdom of the Holy Spirit, and the Holy Spirit both in heaven and on earth is one and the same.

So long as we are on earth we must learn to wage war with the enemy. The hardest thing of all is to subdue the flesh for God's sake, and to overcome self-love.

To overcome self-love we need to be for ever humbling ourselves. This is a mighty science not quickly to be mastered. One must reckon oneself the worst of men, and condemn oneself to hell. In this way is the soul humbled, and the tears of repentance are made to flow which give birth to joy. It is well to school the soul to think, 'I am going to burn in the fires of hell.' But, alas, few understand this. Many there are who despair and fall by the wayside. Their souls sink into a wild state, and then they have no desire to pray or to read or even to think on God.

Man must condemn himself in his soul but not despair of the compassion and love of God. He must acquire a lowly and contrite spirit, and then all intrusive thoughts will depart, and his mind will be purified. But at the same time he must know his own capacity, so as not to overburden his soul. Learn to know yourself, and see to it that your soul's endeavour is within her strength.

Not all souls are equally strong. Some are sturdy as stone, while others are frail as smoke. Those like smoke are the proud souls. As the wind bears smoke hither and thither, so does the enemy draw them whichever way he will, for either they are without patience or else they are easily deceived. But the humble soul keeps the Lord's commandments and stands firm in them like a rock buffeted by the waves. The humble have surrendered themselves to the will of God, and their minds are fixed on Him, and the Lord gives them the grace of the Holy Spirit.

He who lives according to the commandments is aware every hour and minute of grace in his soul. Yet there are people who do not discern the coming of grace.

The man who has come to know the love of God will say to himself: 'I have not kept this commandment. Though I pray day and night, and strive to practise every virtue, still I have failed in the commandment of love towards God. At rare moments only do I arrive at God's commandment, though my soul at all times longs to abide in it.' When irrelevant thoughts intrude into the mind the mind is then concerned both with God and with them, and so the commandment to love God 'with *all* thy mind and *all* thy heart' is not fulfilled. But when the mind is entirely wrapped in God, to the exclusion of every other thought: that is to fulfil the first commandment, though, again, not yet completely.

Train yourself to cut off an intrusive thought immediately. And if you are forgetful and fail to chase them away at once bring God your repentance. Be at pains over this, so that you acquire the habit. The soul is a creature of habit: according to the habit you have acquired, so will you act all the rest of your life.

The love of God has various forms. The man who wrestles with wrong thoughts loves God in his way. He who struggles against sin and asks God to give him strength not to sin, but yet falls into sin again because of his infirmity, and sorrows and repents, has grace in the depths of his soul and mind, but his passions are not yet overcome. But the man who has conquered his passions now knows no conflict: all his concern is to watch himself in all things lest he fall into sin. Grace, great and perceptible, is his.

Thus the soul spends her whole life waging war. But do you not lose heart over the struggle, for the Lord loves a brave fighter.

12

Thoughts on departing from this life

In the body I lie on the earth, but my spirit aspires to behold the Lord in glory. Though I am very sinful the Lord suffered me to know Him by the Holy Spirit, and my soul knows Him, knows how immeasurably merciful He is, and how joyous.

Until the coming of God's grace the soul fears death. She fears God Himself, because she does not know how humble and meek and merciful He is. And there is no man can apprehend the love of Christ if he has not tasted of the grace of the Holy Spirit.

Beloved brethren in the Lord, the merciful Lord is my soul's witness that I write of the truth. And know, brethren—let no one deceive himself—he who does not love his brother does not love God either. The Scriptures speak justly concerning this: fulfil them word for word and you will behold in your own souls the mercy of the Lord, which will take captive the soul, for sweet is the Lord's grace.

The young man seeks a bride for himself and the maiden looks for a bridegroom. This is the earthly order of life, blessed by God. But the soul chosen of the Lord for Himself, the soul He suffers to taste of the sweetness of the love of God, does not set earthly life on a par with the love of God but is absorbed in God alone, and attaches herself to no earthly thing. And if earthly thoughts come to her she takes no delight in them, for she cannot love the things of this earth: all her longing is for the things of heaven.

In death the soul that has come to know the love of God by the Holy Spirit experiences a measure of dread when the Angels bring her before the Lord, since while living in the world she was guilty of sin. But when the soul beholds the Lord she rejoices in His meek and merciful Countenance, and the Lord in the abundance of His gentleness and love remembereth not her sins. One glance at the Lord, and the love of Him will take up its abode in the soul, and from love of God and the sweetness of the Holy Spirit she will be all transformed.

Our fathers have passed from earth to heaven. What do they do there? They dwell in the love of God and contemplate the beauty of His countenance. The beauty of the Lord enthrals every soul in joy and love. This beauty is made known on earth too, but in part only, for our frail bodies are not able to bear perfect love. On earth the Lord gives the soul as much as she may contain, and as much as His loving-kindness wills.

My soul is nigh unto death and longs with a great longing to behold the Lord and be with Him for ever.

The Lord has forgiven me my manifold sins, and by the Holy Spirit has suffered me to know how greatly He loves mankind.

All heaven is in wonder at the Lord's Incarnation—how the Mighty Lord came down to save us sinners, and by His sufferings won for us eternal rest; and the soul has no wish to think on any earthly thing, but is drawn thither where the Lord is.

Dear to the heart are the words of the Lord when the Holy Spirit gives understanding to the soul. A multitude of people followed after Him when He lived on earth, and for many days they were unable to tear themselves from Him but, hungry, listened to His sweet words.

The soul loves the Lord, and everything that hinders her from thinking of God makes her sad. And if the soul so deeply delights here on earth in the Holy Spirit, how much more will she delight there in the other world!

O Lord, how Thou hast loved Thy creature!

Thy soft, gentle gaze the soul can never forget.

My soul, O Lord, is busy day and night with Thee, and I seek Thee. Thy Spirit draws me to seek Thee, and the remembrance of Thee makes glad my mind. My soul came to love Thee, and rejoices that Thou art my God and my Lord, and I yearn after Thee until my heart is filled with tears. And though all in the world be beautiful no earthly thing can occupy my thoughts: my soul desires only the Lord.

There is nought on earth can satisfy the soul that has come to know God: she longs continually for the Lord, and cries:

'My soul yearns after Thee, and I seek Thee with tears.'

The soul from love of the Lord has lost her wits: she sits in silence, with no wish to speak, and looks upon the world with mazed eyes, having no desire for it and seeing it not. And people do not know that she is contemplating her beloved Lord, that the world has been left behind and is forgotten, for there is no sweetness therein.

Thus is it with the soul that has come to know the sweetness of the Holy Spirit.

O Lord give to us this love throughout Thine whole universe.

O Holy Spirit live in our souls, that with one accord we may all glorify the Creator, Father, Son and Holy Spirit.